# Divorce
# Mediation

# Divorce Mediation

## The Constructive New Way to End a Marriage Without Big Legal Bills

Karen L. Schneider & Dr. Myles J. Schneider

ACROPOLIS BOOKS LTD.

WASHINGTON, D.C.

The Marital Mediation Rules are reprinted by permission of the
publisher, from *Structured Mediation in Divorce Settlement* by
O.J. Coogler.(Lexington, Mass.: Lexington Books, D.C. Heath
and Company, copyright 1978, D.C. Heath and Company)

**ACROPOLIS BOOKS, LTD.**
Colortone Building, 2400 17th St., N.W.,
Washington, D.C. 20009

**Printed in the United States of America by**
COLORTONE PRESS
Creative Graphics, Inc.
Washington, D.C. 20009

**Attention: Schools and Corporations**
ACROPOLIS books are available at quantity discounts with
bulk purchase for educational, business, or sales promotional
use. For information, please write to: SPECIAL SALES
DEPARTMENT, ACROPOLIS BOOKS LTD., 2400 17th ST.,
N.W., WASHINGTON, D.C. 20009

**Are there Acropolis Books you want
but cannot find in your local stores?**
You can get any Acropolis book title in print. Simply send title
and retail price, plus 50 cents per copy to cover mailing and
handling costs for each book desired. District of Columbia
residents add applicable sales tax. Enclose check or money
order only, no cash please, to:
ACROPOLIS BOOKS LTD., 2400 17th St., N.W.,
WASHINGTON, D.C. 20009.

**Library of Congress Cataloging in Publication Data**
Schneider, Karen L., 1944-
   Divorce mediation.

   Bibliography: p.
   Includes index.
   1. Divorce mediation—United States. I. Schneider, Myles J.
II. Title.
KF535.S26 1984    346.7301´66    84-2931
ISBN 0-87491-734-4    347.306166

# ACKNOWLEDGMENTS

This book couldn't have been written without the help of Larry Goldstein. He organized, supervised and computerized. His patience and calm nature made him a perfect "mediator" throughout this endeavor.

We also want to acknowledge Kenny Braunstein, C.P.A. for contributing his time and expertise.

Special thanks to Julie Rovner for helping us get this project started.

Thanks to Jeff and Leslye Schneider for their advice, support, and just being there.

Thanks to both our families—for understanding.

Finally, sincere gratitude and appreciation to our publisher, Al Hackl, and also special thanks to Laurie Tag, Kathleen Hughes, Sandy Trupp and the rest of the Acropolis family.

# DEDICATION

This book is dedicated
to our children, Frankie and Sam,
who are still the center
of *both* our lives.

# FOREWORD

**K**aren and Myles Schneider have been very successful in restructuring their family and their lives by courageously following the structured mediation method of family conflict resolution.

They have also been very successful in demonstrating the new cooperative skills they learned to jointly write this book. *Divorce Mediation* is a journal of their personal experience and a critique of structured mediation.

The Family Mediation Association is enthusiastic about the publishing of this book and proud that the Schneiders followed the mediation method developed by the late O.J. Coogler, founder of FMA.

I am impressed with the unique willingness of Karen and Myles to expose their personal journey through divorce with their clear understanding of the mediation method they used. Their sharing will benefit all couples facing divorce.

Betty Henderson Coogler
President, FMA

# CONTENTS

Chapter 1   Analysis of a Dissolving Marriage—
How We Came to Mediation . . . . . . . . . . . . . . . . . 11

Chapter 2   How the Adversarial System Works,
and Doesn't—Mediation as a
Positive Alternative . . . . . . . . . . . . . . . . . . . . . . . . 23

Chapter 3   Pre-Mediation Feelings . . . . . . . . . . . . . . . . . . . . . 31

Chapter 4   A "Peaceful Alternative" . . . . . . . . . . . . . . . . . . . . 41

Chapter 5   Our Mediation—Orientation . . . . . . . . . . . . . . . . . 51

Chapter 6   How to Find a Mediator
and What to Ask . . . . . . . . . . . . . . . . . . . . . . . . . . 63

Chapter 7   Our Mediation—
Custody and Visitation . . . . . . . . . . . . . . . . . . . . . 81

Chapter 8   Negotiation Skills . . . . . . . . . . . . . . . . . . . . . . . . . . 87

Chapter 9   Our Mediation—
General Financial Disclosure . . . . . . . . . . . . . . . . . 97

Chapter 10  Organizing Financial Information . . . . . . . . . . . . . 105

Chapter 11  Our Mediation—
Financial Support . . . . . . . . . . . . . . . . . . . . . . . . . 129

Chapter 12  Completing the Divorce Procedure . . . . . . . . . . . . 137

Chapter 13   Our Mediation—
Preparation and Review of
Draft Agreement . . . . . . . . . . . . . . . . . . . . . . . . . 143

Chapter 14   What You Should Know about
State Divorce Laws . . . . . . . . . . . . . . . . . . . . . . . 149

Chapter 15   Post Mediation—
Completing the Divorce Procedure . . . . . . . . . . . . 165

Chapter 16   The Future of Mediation—
Winning at a Losing Game . . . . . . . . . . . . . . . . . . 173

Footnotes . . . . . . . . . . . . . . . . . . . . . . . . . . . . . . . . . . . . . . . 177

Bibliography . . . . . . . . . . . . . . . . . . . . . . . . . . . . . . . . . . . . . . 178

Appendix   Memorandum of Agreement . . . . . . . . . . . . . . . . . 181
Tax Consultation Memorandum . . . . . . . . . . . . . 184
Custody, Property and
Separation Agreement . . . . . . . . . . . . . . . . . . . . 188
Final Decree of Divorce . . . . . . . . . . . . . . . . . . . . 193
Marital Mediation Rules . . . . . . . . . . . . . . . . . . . . 195

CHAPTER 1

# Analysis of a Dissolving Marriage

## How We Came To Mediation

For better or worse, divorce has become as much a fact of life as marriage in modern American society. More than one million divorces took place in this country last year, and experts predict that this year will see the dissolution of another million couples. For every two marriages that take place today, another marriage is ending.

Since divorce is in its most technical terms the breaking of a legal contract, our society handles it through its legal system. Yet the current legal divorce procedure completely ignores the fact that a divorce is also the breaking of an emotional contract. Lawyers use the adversary process to get the most they can for their client, and often the result is that one half of the couple "wins" and the other "loses." Prolonged and ugly court battles, ultimately decided by a judge who may understand little of the dynamics of the family involved, frequently result in wounds that never heal completely.

### Emotions at Divorce

Of all the emotional changes that we went through and many people go through when getting a divorce, the overriding one is a feeling of loss of control. There is a sense of powerlessness, of trepidation and vulnerability, and of spinning wildly without control. Your entire life has taken a drastic turn. The longer the marriage, the worse the feelings, no matter who wants the divorce. It represents an unbelieveable upheaval.

Our married life had basically been secure and stable (at least that was the illusion we created for the outside world). All of a sudden it was over, and everything that we had worked for within the relationship was also over. When we were faced with the reality that our marriage had failed, we found ourselves trying to deal with the same issues and questions that almost anyone who has been in a similar situation has had to face. You are afraid that you will lose your children, or not be able to see them enough. You wonder if your children will know that you still love them. Will they still love you? You don't know how you will survive financially. Will you lose a lot of money? Can you keep your home? How will you manage alone? Are you as worthless as you feel at that moment?

You are left with the reality that getting out of a marriage is much more difficult than getting into one, and much more costly. What are your options? Up until now most people would probably decide that this was the moment to drop all these heavy burdens into the lap of a good attorney. So into this already emotionally charged scenario comes the "hired gun" to help the two people do battle.

Attorneys are trained to represent their client to the best of their ability within the legal system. These professionals into whose laps we drop our problems at this critical time are not trained to handle one of the most crucial elements of divorce—the emotions that accompany it. These emotions stem from the most powerful and basic human needs, and are the real forces behind the positions we take.

At this shattering time in their lives, people need a trained advisor to guide them through the trauma and to help them make the transition into a new lifestyle. People need some control over the decisions that are being made regarding their lives; yet, in choosing the adversary system, they give up a lot of that control.

## Mediation—An Alternative to the Adversary Approach
Why do people think that two attorneys, with their legal expertise and impersonal judgment, are better qualified to reach an agreement and make decisions that everyone can live with than the two people whose futures are being decided? The answer is they don't realize that there is another way. This other way is called divorce mediation. It is a

rational, structured, proven process whereby divorce does not have to mean exorbitant legal fees, agonizing custody battles, and emotional devastation for one or both parties involved. Instead of putting their futures into the hands of paid combatants, divorce mediation gives a couple whose marriage is ending the chance to design their settlement together, in such a way that both parties are satisfied with the outcome. Instead of pitting husband and wife against each other, mediation is a peaceful technique that promotes a cooperative sharing of power, culminating in most cases in a relationship that is transformed instead of destroyed.

Like all new things, however, divorce mediation has to gain acceptance. We know it can work because we went through it ourselves. In addition, we have spent the past year studying mediation in depth. We have talked to others who have used the process. We have participated in workshops with mediators, attorneys, and therapists, and we have thoroughly reviewed the literature. Perhaps the ultimate proof of our success with the process is that today, only five years after our separation and one and a half years after the official end of our marriage, our present relationship is such that we wanted to write a book together to help others ease their way through the painful processes that accompany the break-up of a marriage.

## Purposes of This Book

This book has three basic purposes: first, it serves as an in-depth guide to mediation (starting with Chapter 2, How the Legal System Works, and Doesn't—Mediation as an Alternative). All the subsequent even-numbered chapters present information about mediation. They cover material that will be useful for the participants to know as they go through the process. Reading over all these even-numbered chapters will give you a relatively complete picture of what mediation is about and how it works.

This self-help book also includes segments designed to help you gather information you will need in the separation/divorce process. This material can be extremely helpful whether you decide to go through with mediation or not. It may even clarify issues still remaining if you are not yet sure you want to get a divorce. Once some of the necessary information has been gathered, Chapter 10, "Organizing Information" provides guidelines on how to figure out present and future financial needs. Also included is guidance on how to gather the material you need to ensure full financial disclosure and for identification of all jointly owned property.

In Chapter 14, "What You Should Know About State Divorce Laws," we review questions about state laws and summarize information about child custody, support payments, potential tax ramifications, and the dynamics of the divorce process.

Interspersed with these technical sections are segments of our own story. We talk about the background leading to our decision to separate and divorce and about our feelings as we lived through the process. We describe our actions and reactions during mediation—the anxiety and the conflicts over money, custody, visitation, and other issues.

We hope that this book will help popularize mediation as an alternative to the adversary system of reaching a separation and divorce agreement. Having been through mediation ourselves, and having studied the shifting trends in how the legal system views its role in divorce and family mediation, we are convinced that our story should be read by anyone contemplating separation or divorce or a revision of an earlier divorce agreement.

At a minimum, this story will tell you about a positive approach to dealing with a very negative situation. Even if you feel this approach is not for you, some of the technical chapters will make you more knowledgeable about divorce and about how to prepare for divorce. This will give you more confidence when dealing with the difficult issues that divorce presents and will help whether an adversarial approach or a mediated approach is used. Mediation is a confidence-building process applied in a confidence-undermining situation. Mediation can result in the construction of a new relationship rather than just the destruction of an old one, both for the adults and for the children involved.

## Is Mediation for You?

Using mediation for divorce is for you if the following apply:

1. You want an orderly, rational, structured way to deal with one of the most frustrating, confusing, chaotic periods of your life.
2. You want to start your new life with some healthy self-esteem and restored order.

3. You want to take control of your own destiny.

4. You want to work cooperatively rather than combatively with your soon-to-be ex-spouse.

5. You both want to work out an agreement that you will both respect and abide by.

6. You want to reduce the turbulence that accompanies many divorces, both for the adults involved and for the children.

7. You want to minimize the adjustment phase from "we" to "I."

8. You want to understand the options you have in settling the four basic areas of conflict typical of a divorce: child custody and visitation, child support, spousal support or alimony, and personal property distribution.

9. You want to make this experience as productive as possible.

10. You both want to be treated as equals and both recognize the rights of the other to come away with a fair settlement.

11. You want to concentrate on your future and leave the past behind.

12. You both want a fair hearing of your feelings so as to defuse the causes of your bitterness, laying it to rest once and for all.

13. You know that the separation or divorce has to be but are unable to face the reality of it.

14. You fear the often cold and impersonal setting of the legal system's approach.

15. You want to build a trusting relationship with your soon-to-be ex-spouse, a relationship that is even more necessary if you have children.

16. You feel vulnerable, and afraid of confronting your spouse, yet you would like to stand up to him or her. You do not want to acquiesce out of weakness, and not get what would ultimately be in your best interests.

17. You feel guilty about leaving or asking for a divorce.

18. You both want as much financial independence and security as can be achieved within the given circumstances.

19. You realize that no one knows more about your situation than you both, and that therefore no one is better qualified to settle the issues than you both if you are given the proper guidance and assistance.

20. You want to have a trained, neutral, caring professional help you—one whose objectives are compatible with yours and whose aim is to help foster a mutually agreeable, jointly developed settlement.

21. You do not want the procedure to drag out interminably.

22. You want to come up with a fair solution and stop the name calling and blaming, concentrating on a constructive approach to a solution.

23. You want a relatively inexpensive, direct method of dissolving the marriage in a mutually satisfactory manner.

24. You realize that starting a new existence can be made easier if you take responsibility for setting up the framework of your new life.

25. You fear the unpredictability of a court-based divorce procedure.

26. You realize that you are the one who must live with your agreement.

We both strongly believe that if a person is contemplating a divorce, she should give serious consideration to using the mediation process. Even if you start out with mediation and come away before completing an agreement, you have lost nothing. If the process turns out to be nonproductive in terms of reaching a signed settlement agreement, you can always revert to the adversary method. In cases where reaching an agreement is difficult, mediation allows for a "cooling off" period to reconsider positions and new alternatives. In this case you can return to mediation at a later date if you both agree. At the very least, you will have gathered some useful information that you will need to know whether you continue with mediation or not. In addition, you may have gained a valuable insight into your spouse's attitudes on various issues to be covered in reaching a separation agreement.

The cost of mediation is limited and defined at the outset; it cannot escalate beyond your control. Also, the length of mediation is limited—if an agreement cannot be reached within a specified period, then the two parties can turn to other approaches such as arbitration to settle specific problems.

This is not the first book written about divorce mediation, but it is the first written by people who have experienced the process themselves—two ordinary people who chose an alternative method, and saw it work. It is the collaboration of two people who managed to work together and grow as individuals even while their old relationship was breaking apart. This book is written with the hope that when others in a similar situation find themselves faced with a decision to get divorced, they will choose to get divorced with dignity.

## Analysis of a Dissolving Marriage

We really never thought it would happen to us. We both knew other people who had gotten divorced. We had read about other divorces, saw divorces in the movies, on television; but how could two caring, sensitive, decent people like us have let this happen?

We first met when we were teenagers. We both have memories of Myles's mother telling him that he was too young to get serious, that he should date other people and not get so involved so soon. Myles remembers feeling it was nothing to worry about, it probably wouldn't last, and he liked being involved with Karen. Karen remembers resenting Myles's mother for several years because of her attempts to control the course of her relationship with Myles. Seven years later, after an on-again, off-again courtship and despite all objections, we were married.

Yet despite knowing each other for twenty years, it was only after having gone through mediation and having acquired new skills that we were able to really talk and listen to each other. We hadn't ever been able to accomplish that in all the years of marriage. We suppose that initially, when things were okay, we either didn't think about it or assumed that we did communicate. As the years went on, especially during the last years, it was obvious that there was no real verbal interaction. We both can't help but wonder how things might have been had we been able to talk to each other. We are not sure we ever would have gotten married, but we believe that if we had, we probably could have made it work. Communication in the truest sense of the word is an essential ingredient in any relationship.

*Myles:* I asked Karen if she thought she understood why we had gotten married in the first place.

*Karen:* My answer is complicated and goes back to long before our marriage. I came from a poor family. I had an adoring father, an unemotional, distant mother, and a very bright, self-sufficient younger brother. We led a quiet life, stayed very much to ourselves, and were not close with the rest of the family. My father had sacrificed his own career for his parents and spent his life struggling for financial stability. I had a wonderful loving relationship with my father. I truly was his "princess." My family was an honest, loving, and stabilizing force in my life. The pain and sacrifice my father endured in efforts to provide the material necessities of life left a strong impression on me and a corresponding need for both familial and financial security.

*Myles:* I came from a large family. My father was a successful physician. Within the family my mother was a dominated woman. Outside, she compensated by being very active in political and religious organizations. Both my parents were highly respected members of the community and very socially active. My brothers and I were close and had a lot of friends and close family ties. There were great parties and large family functions. The family was well-off financially.

*Karen:* My father died when I was nineteen years old. Shortly before his death, Myles and I had broken off our relationship. When my father died, I turned once again to the comfort of Myles's large family. I needed the closeness that his family represented. I needed the emotional support that I could no longer get from my own family. Over the years I had formed a strong bond with both Myles's father and grandfather. They became substitutes for my own lost father. I was the daughter and granddaughter they never had. I was the sister Myles's brothers never had. We didn't realize until many years later how my inclusion in the family had created an inescapable web that made our marriage inevitable. My close relationship with Myles's family made it impossible for Myles to completely break away from their control. It kept me an ever-present figure in his life whether he wanted it that way or not. In many respects I feel I ultimately married Myles as a result of my love for his family. They were very supportive of me, and I had experienced their love. They provided security in their numbers and comfort in their social success. All the things that were missing from my own family life were available through Myles's family.

*Myles:* I had never learned to think or act as an individual. Without my family I had no separate identity. This led me to feel very insecure. I felt vulnerable without them around—I was always part of a package deal. Karen became my security. Over the years, whenever there were problems to overcome, I would feel close to her and seek her support and advice. Was that love? When I didn't need that support, didn't need to lean on her, I didn't really feel close to her at all.

I asked her if she thought she loved me. She said she really thought she had, she was sure she had at one time, though she admitted that my family had a strong influence on her feelings.

She asked me the same question. I was unable to answer. I am not sure I ever really loved her. I remember feeling like the happiest person in the world the day of our marriage. I remember the early years—they seemed happy enough—but still lacking something. I think that in many ways I wasn't capable of experiencing or giving love, though I didn't know it then. I remember the intense feelings of frustration I experienced as a result of my inability to give love unconditionally. I was often angry and caused many intense arguments because of my anger at myself. I had always been controlled by my family, and I blamed them for my inability to be myself. Karen was just an extension of my family, and I transferred that hostility to her. She was now the scolding, denying "mother" I had so resented as a child.

*Karen:* I was always afraid of Myles—not a fear of physical abuse, but I think I sensed that someday he would leave me. I knew I loved Myles more than he ever loved me, yet I had never really been able to be myself around him because of my fear that if he really knew me he wouldn't love me. I was always trying to please him and say and do just what I thought he wanted. I became totally dependent on him for everything. I didn't know what I would do all alone.

Our relationship was always an up-and-down affair. We started seeing each other regularly when we were in high school. It was obvious that our role models as well as our family relationships were worlds apart, yet our relationship seemed to persist. We both lived at home during college, and that too didn't really help us understand the contradictory dependencies we had developed. After years of an on-again off-again relationship, we finally broke up. Now, looking back, it is much easier to see the impact that our different role models had on our relationship.

My father adored my mother and catered to her. He worked hard to please her and tried to give her everything he possibly could. He treated her with respect, love, and gentleness.

*Myles:*  My father was a dominant, "macho" man. He totally ruled our household. He was boss and never hesitated to make that clear to everyone. My mother was very much controlled by him and constantly manipulated and hurt by his power over her. We all catered to his every whim, and he reminded us often that he was in charge.

Since this was the way I had seen my father act, it was the way I expected to act in my own marriage. Everything we did revolved around me. My friends, my college life, my career...I didn't force this on Karen, but there seemed to be some tacit agreement that this was how it should be.

*Karen:*  I didn't know how to ask for something for myself. I was afraid Myles wouldn't approve and that he would leave me. Myles seemed very much in control. He was preparing for his future. He knew where he was going. I was little more than a shadow.

*Myles:*  My future seemed so uncertain. I was insecure and I relied on Karen's judgment to provide direction. My idea of a relationship was to be outwardly chauvinistic, even though I leaned on Karen emotionally. I also liked to be needed. Karen knew I held all the cards—the family, money, hopes for success. Subconsciously I used all this power to dominate Karen and impress on her how dependent she really was.

*Karen:*  I also thought a wife's role was to remain two steps behind her husband, supporting, giving, doing everything for his comfort—I put all my energies into serving one person who was everything to me.

*Myles:*  I felt I needed someone to need me, to be dependent on me for everything. That dependency was power and control. It made me feel important and special. This dependency was what we equated with a happy marriage. From the very beginning, our relationship had a weak foundation. After a few years of marriage the foundation began to crumble. We started to grow apart. Our philosophies and interests lacked any commonality. More problems began to surface, and the differences multiplied.

*Karen:*  The last years of our marriage were particularly painful. I felt isolated, lonely, and vulnerable. I would stare out of the window like a caged animal and ask myself why I was so unhappy. I had two lovely children, a pleasant home in the suburbs, a husband with a rising professional reputation, and enough money to have a comfortable life. It looked like the American dream, but I knew it was all a facade. I was miserable, yet the trappings of the "good life" made me feel confused and guilty about these feelings. How dare I be so down when everything around appeared to be so positive. What more could I want?

*Myles:* I remember how I sensed that we were growing apart. After the boys were born, Karen devoted every waking moment and half the night to them. I loved them too, but I felt totally left out. I was busy trying to build my practice and work hard, an effort that began to consume more and more of my time. After the children were born, our social life came to a halt. It took a long time before Karen was willing to leave the children with a babysitter. There was justification to her concern. We had lost our first child a few years earlier. The impact of that loss was to make Karen overprotective and anxious where the children were concerned.

We started drifting further and further apart. We both knew the marriage was changing, but we chose to hide behind appearances and avoid confrontations. Every once in a while, we would come close to talking about my unhappiness, but Karen couldn't seem to talk to me. I didn't realize how she felt.

*Karen:* I always had trouble talking to Myles—either his remarks would be so hurtful, cause me so much pain, or the fear of his retaliation would prevent me from expressing my emotions. I was always too insecure to really talk to him. I felt he would play on my vulnerability and use the information I offered to hurt me at some other time. He had a way of going for the jugular. I blamed him for everything. I made him responsible for my unhappiness, my lack of entertainment, my loneliness, my need for financial and emotional support. I expected him to carry my load as well as his.

*Myles:* As my professional reputation and practice grew, I worked more and more. I was home less and less. I did this partly because I was trying to build a practice and partly because I was unhappy at home. It became easier and easier to bury myself in my work and avoid the situation at home.

*Karen:* I tried to bury my unhappiness. At first I spent even more time with the children. I wrapped myself up in my mothering role where I knew I was wanted, needed, and loved. Unfortunately, I also avoided thinking about the impact of this behavior on my deteriorating relationship with Myles. I didn't know what to do about that except avoid it. We had ignored almost all the symptoms until it was much too late.

*Myles:* Eventually, I got involved in a few extramarital affairs. Karen found out, but still we chose to stay together and try to go on for the sake of the children.

*Karen:* I was in a great deal of pain, yet I was still trying hard to be rational. I sank deeper and deeper into my mothering role, my escape. I didn't know what else to do. We tried to talk about things, but I was too hurt to open up. It was too late. The trust was gone. Our philosophies of life as well as our needs and wants were no longer the same. We couldn't communicate at all and, in retrospect, perhaps never could.

We both agreed that the marriage was wrong from the start. It was easy to find fault. Finally, we both had had enough. On February 15, 1979, Myles moved out of the house.

CHAPTER 2

# How the Adversary System Works, And Doesn't

## Mediation as a Positive Alternative

Although we have substituted words and theories for battlefield weapons, the adversary system is a form of civilized warfare. The legal system as it is generally applied to divorce is an adversary system that pits husband against wife.

### The Adversary System

Lawyers and Negotiation—The adversary system is based on a win-lose strategy with a winner-take-all philosophy. To win, one has to have a "good" divorce lawyer since it is common knowledge that the side with the best lawyer has a distinct advantage. A top divorce lawyer is sometimes referred to as a "bomber." Generally people who use bombers or hired guns are people who are so hostile and angry that they are out for revenge at all costs. The client is encouraged to be aggressive and go after his own interests without regard for the total family situation or the future ramifications of his actions. "It is possible for the lawyers to negotiate too hard. In pursuit of the best possible agreement for their clients, some lawyers seem to worsen the post marital relationships of their clients and the clients' spouses."[1] The attorney in his attempt to have some bargaining leverage may begin negotiations with absurd demands that alienate the other spouse more thoroughly, causing future interactions to be more stressed than they might have been otherwise.

**Children and Money as Weapons**—If in fact divorce as we currently know it is a battle, then the two most potent weapons in the arsenal are children and money. People coming to an attorney for assistance in fighting the battle are most often confused and angry. They are looking for an ally who will help them get back at their spouse and make her pay for their misdeeds. They want help in using any means necessary. To these ends, children are fair game. For example, stopping or withholding support payments and denying visitation are techniques used by hostile spouses to manipulate the other spouse into giving in to demands for more money or for custody.

**Exacerbation of Conflicts and Painful Emotions**—The unresolved vindictiveness between the spouses is exacerbated by the adversary system. The two people have no opportunity to interact with each other in any positive way. The lawyer becomes the spokesperson for them, and communication between the spouses is discouraged. The paradox is that, although the basis for resolution is direct negotiation, two people must rely on second-hand information.

The legal system has not paid enough attention to the emotional effects of divorce. The actual divorce is not an event that occurs in a courtroom and then is finished. Divorce is a process that sets in motion events that continue long after the legal document is signed. Divorce is significantly more damaging to all concerned when it leaves the parties with continuing battles to be fought. The divorce process is an unknown to most people. It may be the first time that they have been involved with an attorney or with the court system.

The adversary system can make you feel like a spectator when you should be a participant. You are left waiting around for information from two attorneys who are not nearly as concerned as you are with the results. You may spend a lot of time sitting at home or at work agonizing over when to call, whether to call, and how much it costs each time you call. Your anxiety may skyrocket when you contemplate how things are going, when the next battle will be fought, how long will it take, and when it will ever end. At the same time, you are made to feel more and more that someone with whom you may have shared a good part of your life is now your worst enemy. Even if your ex-spouse appears friendly and pleasant, you begin to distrust her actions. You wonder what her strategy is, what she is up to.

The anxiety a person experiences during a divorce will have a significant effect on the person's ability to deal with the process. Generally, lawyers and judges lack training in dealing with the emotional and psychological issues that affect and are affected by divorce. The elevated anxiety level a person experiences may cause her to make unrealistic demands or concessions. Lawyers don't always have the time or background to analyze the history behind a person's decisions.

**Postdivorce Effects**—Moreover, in the adversary system a dependent spouse may transfer dependence to the attorney; when the settlement is over, she is left feeling unprotected and alone. What she failed to realize is that no one protects you forever. She is left unprepared to cope on her own. The result is that the postdivorce period can be crushing. The debilitating hate and anger that have been left unresolved may color a person's life for years. The divorce process has not helped the person develop any skills for assuming responsibility for her future, and it has not helped her let go of the past.

You have the most to gain or lose by not being in control of your own case. Nobody will give it more time and thought than you will. The courts are over-burdened. A judge who doesn't know you, your plans, dreams, needs, relationships, and doesn't have the time to examine your case as thoroughly as you would like, is going to make some very serious long-term decisions for you, if you're not willing to make them for yourselves. The judge will decide what she thinks is in the best interest of your children and your family based on precedents as well as on her own values, and biases. Even if she does not happen to share your values, you will still have to abide by what she decides. You will be presented with a virtual *fait accompli* about which you will have very little to say.

*Karen:* A personal example illustrates the pitfalls of operating through attorneys. I recently spent several hours reading through a proposed agreement with a very well educated friend. She had just received her copy of a proposed settlement in the mail from her husband's attorney. She was frantic. We picked over each paragraph and phrase. She had her own attorney, but like many women she finds the thought of sitting in the lawyer's office while he explains detail after detail embarrassing and frustrating. Asking for explanation after explanation can make anyone feel foolish and inadequate.

After four hours of work (neither one of us is an attorney), although many questions remained unanswered, she felt less afraid of facing her attorney while he explained how others were trying to spell out her life. She had not participated in this contract, and being told what her husband through his lawyer was trying to get from her or to avoid giving her made her angry and resentful. She didn't even understand the words. The document might as well have been in a foreign language. She didn't know whether she was being ripped off in ways she couldn't even imagine. The suspicions and fears that had been planted would grow as they went along. She was already feeling victimized, and the real battle had not even begun.

What happens after the divorce or separation is as significant as drawing up the agreement. Since the divorcing parties do not participate actively in an adversary divorce, they feel little commitment to the results. Both parties feel uneasy, each side harbors a fear that it has been wronged. The mortar cementing the bricks of this new structure is full of holes. Groundwork for dealing with future confrontations has not been provided. The only alternative considered is to go through the courts. Therefore, the prediliction will be to bring all future problems back to the attorneys and to the courts.

**Why Do People Turn to the Adversary System?**—Given the disadvantages of the adversary system, why do most people continue to turn to court intervention in their disputes?

Probably one of the most common reasons is that they are unaware of the alternatives. A second common reason is spite. If one or the other of the parties is out for revenge or out to punish the other person, a courtroom is the perfect arena. Third, for some people, face-to-face contact with a soon-to-be ex-spouse is extremely difficult or even frightening. Fourth, power plays are sometimes carried to an extreme. Threats of a court battle escalate to a point at which one side or the other is pushed to follow through rather than back down once more. Finally, people are often misinformed about the possible results of court battles; they have unrealistic expectations of what they can win or even of what winning means. Some people are more likely than others to take risks, and while the odds are uncertain they feel the gamble for a larger settlement or a smaller payment is worth the try.

## Mediation

The reality of the situation is that it is more difficult and more costly to get out of a marriage than to get into one. So what are your options? There is a way that while not entirely pain-free, is far less costly than hiring two lawyers and going to court—a way that will put you back in control of your life. That way is mediation.

Mediation is a procedure that has been developed over the past ten years to assist people in the dissolution of their marriage. It is a highly structured and organized approach to achieving a divorce settlement. It is a method of identifying conflicts and resolving them through a defined procedure. Mediation is a task-oriented process that relies on problem-solving techniques to help the couple make decisions which are fair to both of them. Agreements created through mediation tend to be more non-traditional than those reached through the adversary process. Each couple designs its settlement to fit its unique situation.

**Background**—Mediation in divorce settlement began about ten years ago in Atlanta, Georgia. O.J. Coogler, an attorney who had experienced his own unpleasant adversary divorce, formulated the concept. He viewed the process of mediation as a method of restructuring the family during separation and divorce, of helping the two people involved move ahead by learning to communicate and deal with conflicts in a productive way. Mediation gives the responsibility for working out their own conflict resolution to the people involved.

Mediation is not therapy and it is not designed to save marriages. Neither does it promote divorce. It is used when a couple has already decided on a divorce. Mediation is responsive to emotions and personal values, and it is concerned with building a workable future relationship for the two people involved. The objective is to develop a framework that helps preserve the strengths of the relationship, particularly as it pertains to parenting, yet also allows the couple to move on to productive and separate lives.

Effective mediation requires communications skills, some general training in the behavioral sciences, and a working knowledge of the principles of negotiation. Mediators are often trained in mental-health-related fields, or work jointly with a therapist during the sessions.

Mediation works toward resolving the emotional divorce as well as the legal divorce, thus helping prepare the couple to cope with their future independent situation. Mediation fosters a cooperative attitude rather than a competitive one. Mediation requires hard work and the desire to achieve some long-range goals. It is a method of cooperative conflict resolution that will not only help the couple through the divorce negotiation, but will give them skills that will assist them in dealing with future conflicts.

Mediation stresses building up each person as a separate, functioning, contributing individual. Since fault-finding, blaming and destructive attacks on the individual are not permitted, and since the issues, not the people, are the focus of the mediation, the process is a constructive rather than destructive method.

The mediation process is structured and predictable. There are guidelines to follow. To relieve stress, unknowns are kept to a minimum. The agenda for each session is planned ahead.

Mediation is predicated on maintaining direct communication between the people involved. The mediator lets the couple know when she is aware they are experiencing stress and anxiety, and constantly looks for opportunities to relieve those feelings. Having the chance to be listened to in a protected forum is one way to relieve those tensions and reduce stress. Open expression of fears and objectives reduces suspicion, allowing each partner to understand the motivations of the other.

Power as a tool is not part of the mediation process. The "win-win" resolution strategy is accepted by both parties.

**How People Feel about the Results of Mediation**—Working through the steps to the agreement may be stressful, but the result is definitely worth the effort. You are left with a sense of achievement and confidence that you may never have experienced before. The self-assurance and the ego boost you experience as a result of having successfully negotiated the end of one phase of your life and the beginning of a new one will give you pride in yourself and proof of your ability to go forward.

Generally people involved in mediation express a high degree of satisfaction with the results. Since both people have a stake in the agreement and they have worked out the solutions together, there is usually little fear that the conditions will not be honored. Reprisals do not generally figure in mediation, since the solutions are felt to be fair to both parties involved. People who use mediation seem to be the least likely to have problems with their agreements and to engage in lawsuits or court battles in the future.

**Mediation Is Family-Oriented**—Perhaps the greatest advantage of mediation lies in the fact that its methods and goals are so much better suited to handling family conflicts, particularly child custody disputes, than the adversary system is. Its goals are family-oriented. The agreements are worked out by both parents in the children's best interest. Mediation helps both adults emerge as strong and functional in their role as parents. This strengthening of individual parenting roles is groundwork central to the children's future adjustment to the divorce. There is a commitment to the goal of making the children the prime focus of the continuing relationship between the two parents, and there is a sense of dignity in having yourselves negotiate the ending of your relationship.

The result is the creation of an environment so much more tension-free, open, and positive that both adults and children can begin to experience a new sense of trust and cooperation while learning to deal with each other more effectively in their new roles. The children can begin to establish a relationship with each parent independently. Everyone has gained something; and the family, although not together, continues to function.

## Table 1: A Comparison Between the Adversary and the Mediated Approach

| Adversary | Mediated |
|---|---|
| Couple abdicates decision-making to lawyer or judge. | Couple takes responsibility for own decisions. |
| Based on win-lose conflict resolution strategy. | Based on win-win conflict resolution strategy. |
| Communication between two people is discouraged. | Communication is the basis on which decisions are made. |
| Lawyers and judges are not trained to handle emotional aspects. | Mediators are often trained in a health field or work with a health professional. |
| Settlement may be imposed by judge. | Couple designs their own settlement with aid of the mediator. |

| Adversary | Mediated |
|---|---|
| Lack of commitment to results because of lack of participation in agreement. | Strong commitment to results because of active participation. |
| Children suffer adverse effects of battles between the parents. | Children's benefit is prime focus of mediation. Good relationship between parents fosters positive adjustment by children. |
| Children may be used as pawns to gain concessions from other side. | The structure of mediation prevents the children from being used as pawns. |
| Confrontation, bitterness and hostility are fostered. | Cooperation and trust are developed. |
| Dissatisfaction with agreement is likely to lead to increased litigation. | Satisfaction with mutually achieved agreement decreases need for future legal confrontation. |
| Aftermath of divorce can be overwhelming because of lack of preparedness for key responsibilities. | Adjustment after divorce is facilitated by practice in planning and taking responsibility for actions. |
| No new communication, negotiation, or problem-solving skills are learned. | Problem-solving, negotiation, and improved communication skills are learned. |
| Unknown length of time for the process, potential for long battles. | Structured sessions and planned agenda, plus established time frame for reaching agreement. |
| Can be very costly depending on how long and complex the process is. | Can cost far less than contested cases because of set time frame and, usually, lack of need for litigation. |
| Power is an important tool, both in hands of participants and of attorneys. | Power, as a force in decision-making, is virtually eliminated since parties must deal as equals. |

CHAPTER 3

# Pre-Mediation Feelings

## Myles

Looking back now to my life just before beginning mediation, I can remember several particularly anxious times; however, nothing that I can recall made me feel so low, so completely alone, or so scared as preparing to proceed with mediation to finalize the divorce.

We had been separated for almost three years; obviously there was a reason it took us so long to reach the decision to legalize our separation and admit that we were heading toward a divorce. We each had our own reasons for not wanting to face reality. It felt like a bad dream. It was hard to believe this was happening. What started out as a temporary, trial separation was ending up a finality. It was one thing to be free for a limited period of time; it was another to face the permanence of ending a relationship that had lasted more than half my life.

Since I was the one who had precipitated this separation, I felt a great deal of pressure. Was this really what I wanted? There had been someone else in my life when this separation began, a cushion for me to fall back on, but that relationship too had ended. There was no longer anyone else. I was really alone. I thought to myself, "What is it you really want?" I was very confused and scared. I had a lot of emotional barriers to deal with.

Going the last yard was the hardest. The reality of what I had started was just beginning to sink in, and that was very frightening. "I cannot possibly go through with this, I'd rather move away—to anywhere but here." I had to force myself to get out of the car in the parking lot and walk to the building where the mediation was to take place. "Maybe I should turn around and go back home. This must be some horrible nightmare. This cannot be me. I cannot believe I'm going in there...." I can recall all of these thoughts and that awful feeling of panic. It has been several years since the start of the end, but that experience still makes me shudder.

Considering what I was doing and my background, it is a wonder I even showed up and was willing at least to try and handle things myself. It is still hard to believe that I went into mediation knowing I couldn't rely on anyone else to fight these battles for me.

The strongest feeling I had was one of failure. I felt that I had failed Karen, my children, my family, even myself. I was brought up to be a "goody-goody"—there was a right way and a wrong way to do things. We (the Schneider Boys) always did everything the "proper" way. It had to be right—there was no in-between. I always tried to do everything the right way. I tried hard to be perfect, to live up to everyone else's standards. If I didn't measure up, I couldn't be happy. I was hard on myself and couldn't forgive myself for having brought about this predicament.

"Nice" guys don't hurt their wives or children. Breaking this rule could scar me for the rest of my life. I would never be the same. Assuming the responsibility for breaking up a family by leaving my wife and children went against everything I stood for in the past. I was very concerned about causing so many different people discomfort. I remember wishing that Karen and I had had a history of violent arguments. I tried to make myself believe that Karen really was a selfish, obnoxious person—too difficult to live with—anything to help justify my actions to myself. I had always thought that people who get divorced must have had at the very least a history of arguments and had probably experienced physical abuse as well. We were two decent people, who never really argued or fought but who had grown apart. I had trouble justifying my decision. I was worried about how others would judge me.

**Children**—I have always had a habit of overreacting to personal problems and, as a result, I have often made things seem much worse than they really were. I tried to convince myself that I had magnified some of my fears, especially when it came to my children. I love them very much and felt that they wouldn't understand. They were only four and six when we first separated. There had been a lot of tension, but we had tried to avoid loud fights or abrasive behavior when they were around. All they knew was that I had left. If I went through with the divorce, they would feel as if I had abandoned them. I feared that my relationship with them was ruined. Many things I had dreamed of doing with them—sharing with them—I would never be able to do. This all gave me a tremendous sense of guilt, of hopeless despair. One thing I always felt I was and always wanted to be was a good father.

There were times when these feelings about my children would make me consider going back home and staying until they were older. However, recalling how trapped and unhappy I felt, and realizing what wasn't there between Karen and me, I knew that such a return was impossible. Still, part of me wanted to just forget the whole divorce idea. I certainly felt that way the day our mediation was to begin.

I also wondered how my children really felt. They went through periods when they would complain of stomachaches for no apparent reason. I would talk to them about the separation between their mother and me, implying that their emotional upset was probably causing their discomfort. Since they weren't able to verbalize their feelings yet, their fears were being translated into physical pain—their way of letting us know they were hurting. The harsh reality of being responsible for doing this to them really got to me. I wondered if they blamed themselves in any way for my leaving. How could those feelings be prevented? Would this affect their feelings of insecurity? Do they worry about being totally abandoned? What will they think about me years from now? Could I ever be happy again knowing that I caused them so much discomfort at such an early period of their lives? The more I thought about this, the worse I would feel, the weaker my convictions would get, the less likely it seemed that I would be able to go through with the final steps.

**Fears of Retaliation**—It was really hard for me to believe that I was in this situation. Now that I had finally pushed Karen this far, what would happen if she changed her mind and decided to go to an attorney? All I could picture was thousands of dollars in legal fees, and I could hear all the accusations that would inevitably come. No matter what the reasons, I had left, and now I would pay.

I could recall hearing about some divorces within my family and remembered how negative everyone was towards the person who instigated the divorce. That person always seemed to get blamed for everything, and to be kept at a distance from the rest of the family.

One particular case involved someone I had loved for most of my life. It was very sad, no one ever gave him a chance to explain his side of the story or listened to his feelings. I felt that I would also be cut off from my family because I was in the wrong.

**Confusion**—In addition, I was petrified by the thought that I would be broke after the divorce was settled. I had had some rough times financially when I was just starting out, and as a result I had an inordinate fear of financial insecurity. I knew deep down that I wanted to take of my children and Karen, but I feared that if Karen got too vindictive or if the separation process got too rough I would really lose. I would be so depleted financially that I wouldn't be able to get started again. I know Karen was aware of my insecurities, and I was concerned about how she would use this knowledge when it came down to negotiating our financial arrangement. I knew that she was very angry at me, and how she would behave was something I couldn't predict.

I tried to get help from both friends and professionals to support my decision to proceed with mediation, but no one had heard of it or had any experience with it. My attorney, my accountant, and other acquaintances all thought I was crazy and was making an awful mistake. They advised me to get a good divorce lawyer and follow the typical adversary process.

Earlier, Karen and I on our own had worked out a temporary agreement concerning the children and finances. We had been using that agreement for almost three years. My attorney and accountant felt I was giving away too much already. They expressed fear that in my guilt-laden state, I would be willing to give away even more than that, more than I could reasonably handle. They were afraid I would agree to terms that I could not meet. That kind of agreement would leave me emotionally and financially bankrupt, and they suspected that at some future time I would resent it and fight back.

I also talked to several good friends and an uncle, all of whom had been through divorce battles. Even they, with all the bitterness, anxiety, and stress they had experienced in their divorces and since, advised me that mediation was a mistake. Based on their past experiences, they questioned how I could be so naive as to rely on Karen to cooperate and work things out. They warned me that she probably already had an attorney, or was considering getting one, and I would really be in for it.

Trying something new is risky under the best of conditions, and at this very trying time, with no one to back me up in my decision, I started to feel extremely depressed. I can still remember waking up day after day feeling as if my world was collapsing. I was on a merry-go-round, but I had no idea when and where it would stop.

There were times just before we went to mediation that Karen and I had our worst arguments. I would go away steaming mad, saying to myself, "The hell with it, let her take me to court. I'll get a lawyer, and I'll teach her—she'll never get as much from me in court...." I used to dare her, taunt her occasionally, to take me to court. I was confident after talking with lawyers and other people that the state divorce laws were pretty rough on women and that I would probably do a lot better in the long run.

By this time I was in such a confused state of mind that I couldn't trust anyone. The last person I thought I could trust was Karen.

Another outward manifestation of my guilt was my living environment. I was living in a squalid little apartment, denying myself any material pleasures. I was punishing myself for my terrible behavior. I had been living on a very small budget and had been what I considered overly generous to Karen so far. I was afraid that this would now be used against me, since I had set a precedent. I was afraid that Karen would make her needs look great and blame me for putting her in a position she never bargained for. I was feeling guilty, anxious, and very vulnerable.

I wondered if it was possible for us to agree on anything. All matters of importance seemed so cloudy at this stage that it seemed impossible that Karen and I would be able to agree on anything. It was even difficult to accept the fact that it really was Karen and I who were the players in this show. There were no stand-ins.

For over ten years we had learned to rely on each other for almost everything, especially when in trouble. Now here we were in trouble with no one to confide in and trust. This added a new level of confusion to an already confused situation. I wanted to confide in Karen as I always had—but that certainly was not a viable alternative.

**Last-Minute Anxieties**—I panicked a few days before the first mediation session, so I called an attorney who was a friend of a friend. He spent a long time with me on the telephone trying to get me to distrust

Karen, trying to convince me that I wouldn't have to give as much as it seemed that I was prepared to give, and encouraging me to try to get away with whatever I could. I was turned off by this attitude. It angered me, and I found myself defending Karen. He didn't really know us or our situation or our past. I could see where the adversary system would lead once it got started.

On the other hand, I was frightened that Karen would go to an attorney and get similar advice. She certainly had no reason to trust me. However, given the antagonistic approach offered as an alternative in the courts, mediation seemed worth a try.

I have never liked the feeling of not being in control of my own life. I suspect that most of us don't. I felt that going to a lawyer and ultimately relying on a judge's decision was in effect, giving up control of something that was too important to my future. I couldn't picture myself in court, unable to express my feelings. Still, I came to the realization that we had to end this limbo we were in—if not for ourselves then at least for the children's sake. It was a period in both our lives where neither had anyone else. This certainly was important to me. One level of guilt was removed—I only had to worry about one relationship.

I felt that if I could only have the strength to stand up for myself and negotiate my own agreement, it would be a turning point in my life. I felt that if this could happen, then something positive might be extracted from all the pain that I felt. As I walked up the stairs to the mediator's office, I fought the urge to scream and run. I finally said to myself, well, you can try, and if it doesn't work out, just get up and walk out. If this approach didn't work, I could get an attorney to do my dirty work, and still go to war. I lost nothing by trying mediation. I also realized that for the first time in my life, in probably the most important decision that I would ever have to make, I was all alone.

## Karen

I can remember how frightened I was when I entered the family mediation center for the first time. Almost all my friends (and especially my lawyer friends) had told me that mediation would be a big mistake. They all said that I could "get everything" if I had a good attorney. There was always somebody that knew somebody that had been awarded houses, cars, alimony for life, percentages of businesses, and all the other just rewards a divorce had to offer. I was so confused, and my confidence and self-image were at such a low point, that a part of me just wanted to dump the whole case in the lap of an attorney and let him take over. I wanted to abdicate all responsibility and be protected and directed.

As I stood outside the mediator's office, I was more prepared to do battle than to negotiate an agreement. The stakes were high, and suddenly I realized that my whole life was going down the tubes. Over and over I found myself saying, "This isn't the way that I had it all planned—where is the happily ever after?"

I was frightened and angry, and feeling very threatened. I had no idea how I would manage on my own. I had supported Myles through the latter part of his professional training and in the early part of his career. Then I had given up my career to care for the children. Where had it all gotten me? What did I have left? How would I earn a living now—how would I start over? I had been raised to believe that a husband is supposed to take care of you forever. I blamed Myles for putting me in this unenviable position. I was lonely, worried, and hostile.

I wondered what I was doing in a mediator's office. I didn't think that Myles and I could possibly negotiate anything. I wanted someone else to fight this battle for me. I guess I was just there to see what this mediation thing was all about. I didn't really think it was for me, but on the other hand, I had known too many women who had spent their whole lives bitter and unhappy after long and costly divorces. I really didn't want to spend my life involved in court battles. I didn't want my children to be pawns in a power game. I didn't want them to spend the rest of their lives shuttling back and forth between two warring parents. I didn't know how to achieve the balance that I felt was necessary, to get all the things that I felt that I was entitled to after twelve years of marriage and yet to maintain a decent relationship with the father of my children.

**I Needed to Change**—As I waited in the hallway, I thought about the circumstances that had led me to this point. I had lived the "Cinderella Syndrome." I had always been taken care of, and now an attorney should take care of me. Why should I struggle through mediation? I began to grasp at familiar stereotypical protective roles: "I'm just a poor defenseless woman." "I'm not capable of handling my own problems." "I need a protector." I had never felt any need to take responsibility for my own life. There was always a man there to do this for me, first my father and then Myles. There was somebody else to blame if things didn't work out the way I hoped. I had a tendency to let things slide. After all, if I didn't take responsibility for making a decision, ultimately someone else would. Being a protected little girl was very comforting. When I was growing up, my father used to say, "You don't need to worry about anything, I'll do all the worrying for you—I'll take care of everything." He really managed to do that—until he died. I looked for Myles to take over then. Did I need someone to take over now?

Intellectually, I knew that I couldn't be an ostrich forever. I could spout the appropriate jargon: as a mature adult there comes a time when you cannot allow the significant decisions of your life to be placed in the hands of others. Yet I didn't know how to take the first steps toward making those decisions.

When I looked over the packet of information about mediation, I sensed that it might be a starting point for me, a way to begin to take some control of my life. My life as I had envisioned it was not going to be. If there was any chance that I could grow from this experience, this might be the way.

**Could I Hold My Own?**—I was terribly frightened. I knew that I had always been intimidated by Myles. I tend to be a very adaptive person, whereas Myles is very rigid. I thought that mediation would only be a microcosm of our relationship. The dynamics of trying to work out something with Myles seemed impossible. Sometimes I think that he has tunnel vision, so that seeing the other side of an issue is next to impossible for him. Control rather than compromise is his style. Mediation would probably be an exercise in futility. If we had been able to agree on things, we probably wouldn't have found ourselves in this predicament. If anybody could get concessions out of Myles, that person would have to be a miracle worker.

I wondered what role power played in mediation. I had always felt so powerless around Myles that I was convinced that my conciliatory nature would cause me to give in. Myles would just walk away the winner. I figured that he had been advised to give me as little as possible. I knew he would not be sensitive to my fears for the future. He had never seemed to hear me before, why should things be different now? Maybe he would try to get the kids and the house, and would manipulate things so that he would not have to pay me very much. I had no immediate means of support. I had not worked in eight years, my job skills were minimal, and my morale was so low that I couldn't see who would be interested in hiring me for anything. I had given up my career plans when we got married. Myles had even managed to devalue my role as a mother by constantly comparing me negatively to other women he knew who *worked*. Mothering was not worth very much in his eyes. How could I ever establish a value for those past compromises? Could I possibly walk away from this marriage more demeaned than I already was?

I needed a way of finding out who I was—separate from Myles. I needed to define my needs and my goals. Mediation seemed to offer the opportunity to do just that. It was a time of stress and confusion and a time for restructuring. I knew that I had to be involved, not just peripherally, but intimately, in planning the rest of my life. I didn't know if I could stand up to Myles in a face-to-face confrontation, whether it was about philosophies or about practical matters like financial arrangements, but I did know that if it all became too overpowering I could always walk out. I always had the option of placing control back into the hands of an attorney and letting the judge and the lawyers decide the issues.

I knew there was no turning back. I didn't want to go back, even if that had been an option. Sometimes, whenever the fear of being on my own and the fear of not having enough money became vivid again, I wavered. But I couldn't allow myself to be treated like a doormat anymore. Sure, mediation seemed risky, but there are no guarantees in any situation. If I had been asked some years ago if I had thought my marriage would last forever, I would have been the first one to guarantee that it would. I know better now. After Myles had moved out and I was forced to begin to take charge, I didn't want to backslide into that protected little girl role again. Mediation was an opportunity to do something about it. At least I had to try.

## CHAPTER 4

# Mediation

## A "Peaceful Alternative"

**A** divorce agreement achieved through marital mediation, or structured marital mediation, is not only a viable, but actually a preferable alternative to one created by the legal/adversary system most often used today. Mediation is not aimed at saving a marriage; its sole purpose is to effect a productive and workable separation and divorce. Unlike the legal system, it can provide a way in which the divorcing couple can participate directly in making the decisions that will affect their lives.

Mediation does not attempt to eliminate all conflict, since conflict is an important component of problem resolution. Unlike the legal process, however, in which conflict may be destructive in that at least one party will feel they have lost, mediation seeks to make conflict constructive so that both participants are satisfied with the outcome and feel they have gained.

In the legal/adversary approach, divorce is by definition a destructive process—a breaking of a contract. As a result, the situation is usually viewed in an "I win, you lose" context. This can create anger and bitterness. In mediation, on the other hand, the premise is not to label either person guilty but to accept that no one is better able to understand what actually happened to a marriage than the participants. Mediation forces both people to take responsibility for negotiating their own futures. It doesn't focus on who wanted the divorce or who did what to whom. The divorce is going to become a reality for both partners no matter who initiated it.

By negotiating themselves, both spouses become less confused about the impending divorce. As each partner assumes greater responsibility in the negotiation process, emotional turbulence is diminished.

This shortens the postdivorce adjustment period, since each person tends to come away with an increased feeling of self-respect and dignity, as well as with more respect for the feelings and needs of the ex-spouse.

## Aftereffects of Mediation

Mediation can actually produce positive results from what appears at the outset to be a totally negative situation. It has been shown that if people actively participated in coming to an agreement, they will be much more likely to live up to its terms. Statistics show that people involved in mediated settlements tend to comply more often with the terms of payment and visitation than in court-settled divorces.

Mediation fosters a cooperative attitude rather than a competitive one. It is designed so that both sides can gain something from the final outcome. This is important not only for getting through the divorce itself, but also for the future of the relationship, and there is a future when there are children involved. Each party will have to deal with the other for many years after the divorce is final, so it is certainly an advantage if people can achieve their goals while remaining decent and civil toward each other during and after the divorce process. The "win-win" atmosphere (I get something, you get something) helps the two people deal with each other in a more cooperative and constructive way throughout the remainder of their lives.

Structured mediation is based on a set of marital mediation rules which are used as a guide toward dissolving a marriage. These rules, which encompass all major issues involved in divorce and which require the active participation of both partners, were formulated by the Family Mediation Association, a national organization whose purpose is to promote marital mediation as an alternative to the legal adversarial process. The FMA based its rules on divorce laws from some of the more progressive states, as well as on its own research on divorce results. The result is a set of guidelines well ahead of even the most up-to-date state laws. The document drawn up as the result of a mediated settlement is a legal separation agreement which can be used as part of a legal divorce decree.

As stated before, mediation is not a way to mend a failing marriage. What it can do is provide two people who have already decided to get a divorce with an impartial third party who can help them separate the issues from the guilt and egos involved as much as possible. The mediator's role is to direct the participants through the various issues that need to be addressed before the divorce can be finalized.

## Who Assists the Couple?

A *mediator* may be a psychologist, psychiatrist, marital counselor, therapist, family therapist, or an attorney who may have undergone special training by the Family Mediation Association. In addition to the mediator, *an advisory attorney* may be called in to look over the final agreement and put it into a form that will stand up in court and be recognized as a divorce decree, if the parties so desire. The advisory attorney can also give impartial legal advice to each party and ensure that they understand the legal ramifications of what they have agreed to. An *independent accountant or tax attorney* is often consulted as well, to give recommendations on how to handle the financial aspects of the agreement to the mutual benefit of both parties, and to clarify all the financial and tax implications of the agreement.

## Areas of Contention

The actual process of mediation deals with the four major areas of contention that must be resolved to settle divorce questions:

1. Divisions of marital property
2. Alimony or spousal support
3. Child support
4. Child custody arrangement

These areas need not be handled in the order listed above, but in whatever order best meets the participants' needs. The order presented is that which is preferred for most situations by the Family Mediation Association.

It is important that the focus during mediation always remains on the issues. Individual emotional problems are very much a part of the divorce process, and they are dealt with when indicated. As with substantive issues, emotional issues are handled by the mediator in a way which fosters individual growth, but these issues are not allowed to bog down the process. The mediator is trained to understand and deal with the emotional side of divorce, but she is also trained to separate the emotions from the substantive issues and the issues from the people involved.

The mediator begins by seeing that all the agreed-on issues are brought up, settled, and out of the way in as little time as possible. This approach limits the number of future potential problems. It also enables the mediator to praise the parties and start to build a sense of accomplishment and cooperativeness between the participants. If they can initially focus on things they agree on, they can soon begin to see the potential for working out other issues as well.

Marital Property—The first step in this process is to define what the term marital property includes. This requires each participant to provide certain financial data and income statements. It also includes filling out detailed monthly and yearly budgets as well as projected future financial needs. The mediator provides forms to aid the couple and help elicit necessary information. When the information is analyzed, a fairly exact idea of what the couple owns and what they need can be determined.

The next step is dividing the property equitably. The process of property division illustrates another significant advantage of mediation over the standard legal adversary approach. In court, if I get something, that means you don't. In mediation, however, the pie can be divided to the best advantage of all involved, and one person's gain does not necessarily mean another person's loss.

There are basically three ways to divide marital property:

- *Division in kind* in which "I get this and you get that."
- Maintaining *joint ownership*, which may be advantageous for real estate or small business holdings where another partnership or business arrangement is involved.
- *Selling* the property for a predetermined sales price with a predetermined split of the profit or cash from the transaction.

Once you have figured out what the property is, you have to decide who gets how much. While many states provide that property shall be split 50/50, this is not the case in mediation. Although mediation does recommend a 50/50 split as a rational beginning point, each situation is dealt with according to its own merits. Then, depending on the needs of the people involved, appropriate adjustments can be made. Factors considered in determining the split include:

- The contribution of each spouse to the acquisition of the property. If one spouse is a homemaker, that spouse should not, however, be penalized for not accumulating financial worth.

- The housing needs of the people involved.
- Property that was owned solely by one party before the marriage.
- Any frozen assets such as money tied up in long-term investments or stocks which may not be salable at the time of the separation. In this situation, the couple must work out a system to achieve future division of their holdings, while retaining joint ownership until a more suitable time to sell is determined.
- The advantage, if any, of paying more money to the dependent spouse in exchange for an unequal split of the accumulated property.

**Alimony, or Spousal Support**—The next issue is to determine the amount of alimony to be paid to the dependent spouse. First, it must be decided which spouse is the dependent one; then the amount must be determined. It will vary depending on several factors:

- The realization that both lifestyles will have to change . Maintaining two households requires that both parties make some significant adjustments.
- The length of the marriage.
- The physical and emotional state of the dependent spouse.
- Various needs of the dependent spouse, including the financial potential of the supporting spouse and her ability to meet the above needs.

The idea of mediation is to prepare both people for an independent future. For the dependent spouse, this usually means planning a new career or learning new skills to become self-supporting. This readjustment period often requires that extra financial support, known as *rehabilitative support*, be provided for a predetermined period of time. This encourages the dependent spouse to work gradually but steadily toward self-sufficiency.

It is often advantageous to include child support under the heading of alimony to give a tax break to the supporting spouse. She, in turn, can share this break with the dependent spouse by being more generous in support payments.

**Child Support**—Child support must be settled before dealing with child custody. Often child custody is used to enhance one side's bargaining position, disguising it in statements like "I want what's best for the children," and "what's best for the children is for them to live with me." By settling the financial matters first, including child support, children won't be used later as a bargaining chip. This is extremely important.

Until recently, it was almost universally thought that the man should be responsible for all child support. But that is changing rapidly, and marital mediators are very much aware of the unfairness of such a generalization. While child support is definitely to be considered a joint responsibility, sometimes the supporting spouse will initially carry a heavier burden that will diminish over time as the dependent spouse becomes more financially independent. As the two incomes approach equality, the support payment for children may be altered. Other variables to consider include:

- The amount of money that the custodial parent will be able to contribute.
- The amount that the supporting parent can realistically supply.
- The financial needs of both parties, independent of the children.
- Inherited money that the children may have, and their ability to work and contribute, if not immediately then after a given period.
- Any physical or emotional problems requiring special care for one or more children.
- Health and life insurance factors.

**Child Custody**—Child custody is frequently the last issue, since it is often an area of considerable controversy. If the mediator expects problems, she sees to it that, prior to dealing with this issue, all previously settled issues may be put into a legal document and signed by both parties. This helps eliminate the use of the children as pawns by either side to gain a financial advantage. If there is competition for the children, important factors to consider include:

- What would be best for the stability of the children.
- The emotional ties between children and the competing parents.
- The capacity of the competing parents to give the children the love and guidance they need.

- The kind of home situation that the custodial parent will be able to offer the children.
- The various home, school, and community needs of the children.
- The opinion, if applicable, of the children themselves.

Sometimes the children are included in mediation to ensure that they understand what is happening to the family. Many parents do not realize that children can handle divorce a lot better if they know what is going on. Openly discussing the situation with them at least, if not including them in one or more of the mediation sessions, can go a long way towards avoiding unnecessary anxieties.

Options with respect to child custody include sole custody, joint custody, and shared living arrangements. It is even possible to use one house and have the parents move in and out. This is often referred to as "nesting." In mediation, special care is given to make sure that the best interests of the children remain the primary concern.

## Orientation Session

A basic format has been designed as part of the mediation procedure in order to get through the issues described above. The first step is the orientation session. Before this, both parties receive a packet of materials including a description of mediation, the rules and guidelines, necessary forms, and monthly financial data sheets to be filled out. Participants are given ample time to go over the material before the orientation meeting. This session is held at the place where the actual mediation will occur.

Orientation begins with a review of the material in the packet. Questions are answered, and the mediator makes sure that the participants fully understand the process. Next, both parties usually sign a document stating that they agree to mediate this divorce, that they understand all issues involved in the process and are willing to abide by the rules. Included in the agreement are a suggested preliminary schedule for the meetings with the mediator, as well as a predetermined date by which the mediation will be completed. A date for the initial mediation session is then set.

Unlike the legal/adversary approach, mediation does not allow the painful process to drag on. If, after 10-14 hours of negotiations or less, a final settlement is not reached (which is rare), the couple either isn't ready to finish the divorce process, goes to arbitration, or is told to stop mediation for a time and, if they choose, return at a later date.

**Impasses**—If the parties reach an impasse over an issue, the mediator can recommend tht the particular issue be settled through arbitration. A stipulation that an impartial arbitrator mutually agreed on may be used to settle such problems is included within the rules of mediation. This person may be picked from the American Arbitration Association or may be a neutral third party acceptable to both people. According to mediation rules and the law, the arbitrator's decision is final and may not be appealed. It will also be upheld in a court of law. While our research indicated that use of arbitration is rare, it does serve the purpose of preventing one party or the other from using an impasse as a strategy for bargaining power.

**Fees**—Also discussed during the orientation session are fees. A deposit is usually made according to the payment plan or the rules of the particular meditor or mediation center. Expect to pay between $400 and $600 for the mediator; from $200 to $500 for the advisory attorney; and between $300 to $500 for the tax consultant. Mediators usually require a percentage of the payment for at least the mediation sessions in advance. The advisory attorney, tax specialist, and other additional advisors are usually paid when services are rendered.

Prepayment of the mediator helps establish a commitment from both parties to complete all the sessions. Mediation requires that both people share equally in the cost. This approach is in keeping with the philosophy of mediation, which requires shared responsibility for all aspects of the divorce process. Obviously, each mediation center, association, or individual mediator may have different arrangements for payment.

**Other Orientation Session Activities**—During the orientation, the mediator tries to get some background information about the two people as individuals, including their description of how they decided to use structured mediation. She also tries to determine at this time whether or not there may be a custody problem. Additional issues or information may also be furnished by the participants. At the conclusion of the orientation, the mediator should be able to formulate an agenda of issues to be settled and the order in which those issues will be considered. Finally, the mediator gives out and goes over financial data and personal information sheets to be filled out by the parties.

These include, in addition to what has already been mentioned, provision for possible emergency expenses, seasonal expenses, installment debt payments, analyses of family expenditures, and any predivorce agreements.

The actual mediation sessions are generally planned about a week or two in advance and are usually scheduled to last from one and a half to two hours. There are other ways to handle this; those alternatives will be discussed in later chapters. Our research showed that the average time for the process was five to seven two-hour sessions. (This does not include several hours of work done by the advisory attorney and tax specialist or tax consultant.)

## First Session

At the outset of the first session, the rules are reviewed again to ensure complete understanding and agreement by both parties, giving the mediator a chance to compliment both on their ability to cooperate and agree on something.

Then the proposed agenda is presented. The typical order of issues to be resolved is as follows:

1. Temporary support and custodial agreement. These are not permanent nor binding, but only a means of achieving an initial stage of stability.
2. Identification and division of property.
3. Alimony.
4. Child support and visitation rights.
5. Child custody.

The agenda may be changed by the mediator depending on the individuals involved and their given situations.

## Later Sessions

Usually all the issues have been settled by the end of the sixth hour. By the seventh hour, the advisory attorney is called into the sessions for the first time. She answers any legal questions, then reviews the unofficial agreements before drafting them into proper legal language. The drafts are mailed to the couple before the next session, when they are reviewed by all parties. Between these two meetings, a tax specialist will also be contacted to lend her expertise to the settlement process (if she hasn't already been consulted, which is often the case).

After the agreement is carefully reviewed by the two individuals, each has the option of going to separate attorneys and accountants for independent opinions. If this is done and any needed adjustments made, the couple goes to the advisory attorney's office to sign the document, which, after being notarized, is considered legal and binding. After the appropriate separation period, this document may then be filed as a formal divorce decree.

## Functions of Mediation

Thus, the mediation process fulfills several functions. It can be used

- To formulate a temporary separation agreement while the complete agreement is being worked out.
- To work out the final legal separation.
- To prepare a document that can, after the appropriate separation period, be filed as a legal divorce decree.
- To revise a previously settled divorce decree or legal separation agreement. This revision may have to do with financial needs, with the needs of the children, or with some new development for one or both of the people involved. It does not matter whether the initial settlement was accomplished through the standard legal process or by other means.

CHAPTER 5

# Orientation

## Our Mediation

**S**everal weeks before the first mediation session, we were given pre-orientation packets by the family therapist we had been working with during our separation. We were supposed to read the material and familiarize ourselves with the concept and the process of mediation. The therapist encouraged us to talk about it together to be sure it was what we really wanted to do. The packet contained information about mediation and how it works, sample forms, and a mediation agreement which we were both to sign before beginning the sessions.

We both read over the literature and felt it looked like something that could work for us. Our lives seemed out of our control—we were spinning around, waiting for the wheel of misfortune to stop.

We had been separated for some time and were really stuck in limbo, each for different reasons. Karen still had not given up hope of a reconciliation. Myles was guilt-ridden, especially about the children, and could not get himself to finish what he had started. Myles was also afraid of the financial ramifications of a divorce settlement, and this fear contributed to his inability to move forward. Neither of us was really facing reality.

Divorce, although inevitable, was still not comforting, in spite of all the difficulties we had been through. It represented a finality neither of us was willing to pursue. We were afraid of getting entangled in the legal system. We seemed to sense that taking our case to the courts would leave us bitter enemies, a situation that would be intolerable for our children. Despite all our personal conflicts, we were both committed to the need to maintain a decent level of stability for our children. Their welfare was perhaps the one common link we retained. This need was what gave us the courage to try a different way to proceed with the divorce.

When we read that one of the basic objectives of mediation was to help the individuals involved become independent, emotionally and financially, by having them work out their own agreement, something in each of us responded positively. For Karen the process offered a means of gaining independence, and through that independence a sense of security when all security had been yanked away. To accomplish this, she first had to be able to overcome her anxiety about facing Myles directly. She had to establish control, and at least in part take it from Myles. That push for control, if it could be accomplished, would be a first step in a new life. Myles, on the other hand, felt that mediation offered him a means of retaining control, by not having to relinquish that control to the court. It meant not having to deal with Karen's lawyer. If she did not have an outside protector, he felt that he could dominate her in a confrontation as he always had in the past.

Nevertheless, it was still a formidable task to walk through the door and begin mediation. We had nobody to turn to who had already been through it, nobody with whom to compare notes. We did not know any other couples who had mediated their own divorce. Even looking back on it now, without the intense anxiety that we both felt at the time, it is difficult to imagine what we expected. How would we work out our own divorce, when we certainly could not work anything else out together?

## First Session

The therapist, Karen, and Myles arrived separately and were seated in the waiting room of the mediator's office. After a few minutes, the mediator's secretary asked us all into what turned out to be a typical lawyer's office conference room. It was a long narrow room with wall-to-wall bookshelves filled with law books.

The mediator was already there, standing at the head of the table. He suggested Karen sit to his left and Myles to his right. This had the effect of forcing us to face each other right from the beginning. The therapist sat at the far end of the table.

The mediator immediately set an informal tone to the proceedings with his easy-going manner. He welcomed us and told us a little about himself. He was an experienced lawyer, specializing in family, hence divorce, law. He had been divorced via the traditional adversarial system years before, and he had a child of his own. His personal and professional background led him to an interest in mediation, and he had been mediating divorces for several years. He further explained to us that having gone through a divorce himself, he was very familiar with some of the emotions we were feeling. His approach succeeded in having a soothing effect on both of us.

The therapist, who had been working with us previously as well as with the mediator, was herself training to be a mediator. She too had been divorced via the legal system and realized its shortcomings. She was motivated by her past personal and professional experiences to become more directly involved in mediation. She was involved in our mediation primarily to get additional experience. She also had a personal interest in our efforts, as a friend and as a therapist to both of us. Finally, she knew a good deal about us and would make sure we both expressed our anger and frustrations directly. She was very much aware of Karen's fear of Myles's dominance, of Myles's use of this fear to maintain control, and of Myles's guilt.

So here we were, probably at the most stressful point in our lives, placing our futures in the hands of a process we only barely understood. We were looking for help and guidance from two professionals who both had experienced what we were going through. Despite the fact that this was only our first meeting, the mediator seemed to convey a feeling of understanding and empathy for each of us as individuals. Although we were both still very nervous and confused, within minutes we were a lot more relaxed and hopeful about our decision to try mediation.

We were in neutral and physically comfortable surroundings. This was no cold and austere courtroom. The two people who were present were not representing either one of us against the other, but were working with both of us to help us work out our problems together, so we could have a more positive future, independent from each other.

The mediator asked us to explain why we thought we were there and how we had arrived at our decision to seek a divorce. He wanted to hear the background from each of us. He listened, allowing us both the opportunity to express ourselves without interruption. This was his way of breaking the ice, of sizing us up, of seeing how we interacted with each other, of understanding something about us and where we were coming from. We were sure that the therapist had told him what she knew about us, but he needed to establish his own interpretation of the dynamics of our relationship. He summarized what each of us had said, which helped us hear what we each had said more clearly, and to identify our positons and problems with some level of objectivity.

After we reviewed our story with him, he asked us if we were in agreement that a divorce was the way to proceed. We both said yes. He then explained that we were all there to prepare a separation agreement that could ultimately become a final divorce decree. His main role was to help us negotiate the separation agreement in a positive way, so that each of us would be better prepared to handle new future roles independently.

He explained to us that in mediation, the idea is that no one wins at the expense of the other. There are no losers in mediation. We would be working toward a mutually agreeable solution of the various issues involved in our divorce. We would formulate an acceptable agreement together and its implementation would be our mutual responsibility. His function as a mediator was to guide us through the issues in an organized way. He would help us identify areas of agreement, set reasonable limits for us, and help each of us define and clarify our positions.

The mediator would remain impartial. He had no power or authority over us. Although he was a lawyer, he would act only as a mediator and would not give either one of us legal advice. He would not make decisions for us, and he would be there primarily to help us work out our conflicts ourselves.

## Rules
He went over some basic rules. They essentially were that, as we began to negotiate each issue, both of us would be expected and encouraged to say what we thought and what we felt, no matter what. There would be enough time to do this. The other person was supposed to listen and not interrupt in any way. In addition, the mediator wanted to remind us of several points:

1. If either of us was completely dissatisfied, we could bail out, and that was that.
2. If one or both of us wanted an extended period between sessions for a valid reason, then a suspension of the process for a controlled period would be arranged.

3. If we came to an impasse, then the issue causing it would be submitted to a mutually approved arbitrator and her findings would be binding.

4. If we wanted to consult independent attorneys or accountants at anytime, we were free to do so.

The mediator reminded us that mediation is a process that relies on cooperation, and that it provides an alternative to the adversary process, which often results in increased hostility and bitterness. Mediation, on the other hand, places the responsibility for making decisions with the two people involved. It works toward the creation of a viable separation agreement. Finally, he pointed out to us that the key to successful mediation is trust. Since we obviously didn't trust each other very much right then, we needed to be able to trust some neutral party (the mediator) to help us resolve our conflicts. What we decided to do about the details of our separation was our decision. He would not make decisions for us, but he would tell us if he thought either of us was being unfair or unrealistic.

## Issues to be Dealt With

We were then asked if we had any questions. Then we proceeded to a general discussion of the issues that would be dealt with as part of the mediation. As we listened to the mediator, each of us could see that if we could work this through, we could have some pride in ourselves for being able to regain control over our situation at a time when it seemed as if everything was falling apart.

The mediator then discussed with us the four areas which would have to be settled as part of the separation agreement: child custody and visitation, child support, division of property, and alimony or spousal support.

He asked us to tell him what we thought would be the areas of least and most contentions. We both had our chance to speak, and the gist of our discussion was agreement on the fact that the issue of child custody and visitation would be the subject of least contention. We also felt that property division would be our most difficult problem, since we were both insecure about our future financial condition. The issues of child support and alimony were potential disasters because what Myles thought Karen should get was very different from what Karen thought she needed to get her life in order again.

## First Steps

We did reach a preliminary understanding from this first meeting that
Myles did intend to take care of the children financially and that he
did understand and feel he had an obligation to support Karen financially at least for awhile. It was obvious, however, even though no
figures had yet been discussed, that Myles and Karen would have difficulty agreeing on what amount was adequate. Each had radically different viewpoints on what was meant by *need*.

The mediator immediately pointed out to us the positive aspects of
our first efforts in this mediation. We both had at least agreed on which
areas we would probably be able to agree about and which areas would
probably give us difficulty. That may not sound like much, but it surprised us that we were able to agree on anything at all.

Using an easel and chart paper for visual impact, the mediator then
wrote out his suggested agenda. He suggested starting with the areas
in which we had a better chance of reaching agreement. This approach
would help us learn to deal directly with each other and become accustomed to the mediation process. This way, we would get in touch
with our strengths before we started to go over the financial areas where
we expected real problems. This was particularly important for Karen.

## Agenda

We decided to take up the four major areas in the following order:

1. Child custody and visitation.
2. Financial disclosure and division of marital property.
3. Child support.
4. Spousal support.

Again, we were able to agree on something—the agenda. Any agreement was viewed as a significant accomplishment. We may never have
felt like cheering about an agenda before, but to us it was a promising
step.

During these exchanges, the mediator was getting to know us by
watching and listening, all the time evaluating our manner of inter-
acting. It was obvious Karen had to be coaxed to speak out more, that
Myles was more talkative than she. He was used to dominating their
discussions, especially during arguments. These factors were to play
an important part in all future sessions.

In addition, we could now get an idea of the potential cost of the mediation sessions. The mediator was able to come up with some estimates based on his past experience and on our explanations and apparent disagreements.

We were told that the sessions would each last two hours and would be scheduled one or two weeks apart at most. They would cost $120 per session, and this would include both the mediator's and the therapist's fees. The mediator estimated the need for four or five two-hour sessions to complete the separation agreement. We were further told that he would advise us to see an independent tax consultant during the process; the charges for that were estimated at $60 per hour. We would need to allow some additional hours with the tax consultant to work out the details of our financial agreement once we had agreed to the basic elements. This final agreement would take into account our individual advantages from a tax standpoint and would help us meet our future financial needs.

There would also be a need for a few hours of the mediator's time to write out our preliminary separation agreement, after the sessions were all over and he had received the tax consultant's report. Finally, independent of our sessions, we would be referred to an advisory attorney to rewrite the agreement into proper legal form. Whenever we chose to turn the legal separation into a divorce, we would also need to have an attorney file for us.

The mediator then reviewed the total estimated costs. They were expected to fall between $1,500 and $2,000 for all services, including those of the filing attorney, and including other requisite divorce fees. Considering our situation and what we knew to be the much higher costs paid by friends and relatives who had gone through adversarial divorce proceedings, the estimated mediation costs seemed both fair and reasonable. To ensure cooperation and commitment to the mediation process, each of us was to be held responsible for one-half of the total costs.

We were then each given several forms dealing with financial matters to review. They included financial information and income statements, and monthly expense budgets covering present and future expenses and existing liabilities. We were expected to have these forms completely filled out by the third session, which was intended for dealing with financial matters. In addition, Myles was to furnish tax returns for the previous two or three years plus a list of all investments and property accumulated up to that point.

Finally, both the mediator and the therapist congratulated us again on accomplishing a great deal in our first session. They also told us they both realized we were still insecure with the process and that there would be days between now and the end of the sessions when it would seem as if it would all work out, and there would be other days when we would feel just the opposite. We were admonished not to worry about such feelings, that they were normal for all couples going through a divorce. The mediator indicated that we should feel free to call him or the therapist between this and the next session if we had additional questions. They did advise us against discussing the mediation issues with close mutual friends or relatives, saying that to do so would only complicate matters, possibly leading to confusion and more severe problems. Later experience demonstrated how right they were.

Last, but certainly not least, the mediator advised us that we were free to have independent attorneys and accountants review what was happening at the sessions. As a matter of fact, he mentioned this often during our sessions. He also reiterated that if either of us became dissatisfied or came to the conclusion that mediation was not for us, then we could walk out and that the results of the process would not be binding. He reminded us, however, that if we opted to go with an adversary divorce, we would be leaving all the decisions to the lawyers and the judges. We would be subject to accepting somebody else's decisions. He asked whether we felt that the location for the sessions was reasonably convenient and accessible to both of us. We both answered affirmatively. Then a date for the next session was set for approximately two weeks later.

After leaving the session, we both were still unsure that we were doing the right thing by using mediation. We were still confused and anxious but we realized that we had both participated in an important event and that at least we were trying to control our future. We had managed to break our old patterns, and this by itself was important to both of us.

## Reactions

*Myles:* I liked the mediator. I felt comfortable with him because he was male, because he had experienced the negative side of divorce through an adversary process, and because he was a professional who, if he were in the same position as I, would also have a lot to lose. Therefore, he more than likely would be able to empathize with me and understand my concerns. I had by this time developed a trust and respect for the therapist, both as a friend who cared for my well-being and as a professional. I also found the mediator's calmness and proficient manner of handling the session very comforting. The informality and the physical comfort of the surroundings contributed to my sense of security, helping to offset the anxiety of the moment.

I also liked most of what the mediation process stood for. I felt good about the goals that were outlined, particularly in reference to striving to make Karen emotionally and financially independent. In addition, I was pleased to find out that the cost would not be prohibitive, and that Karen would be responsible for paying half.

On the other hand, the reality of actually going through with the divorce had finally begun to sink in. It was a frightening experience. I had trouble coping with the ever-present guilt and the feelings of self-incrimination. During the entire session, Karen was busy taking notes, as she would continue to do during the entire process. This unnerved me, and led me to believe she was under the guidance of an outside attorney, using these sessions to try to get as much information out of me as possible. I wondered if I was being foolish in feeling I could trust her, especially when it came time for my financial disclosure. I wondered if I shouldn't consult an outside attorney at this time. Finally, the fact that if we became deadlocked, we had agreed to submit that issue to binding arbitration made me very nervous. The saving grace was that I could always walk out if things didn't go my way.

*Karen:* I had similar feelings about the physical surroundings and had also begun to develop a sense of trust in both the mediator and the process. I felt that since the therapist was a woman, I might ultimately have an ally. The fact that the therapist who had experienced an adversary divorce and was training to start a career of her own, led me to believe that she would empathize with me and understand my fears.

As far as the mediator was concerned, I felt confident because he was in control—feelings I needed because of my fear of Myles's ability to take over any situation in which we were involved as a couple. The mediator appeared to be impartial, which tended to calm my fears. I was always afraid of Myles's domination during arguments when we were married. I had my doubts about being able to stand up to him on my own without a lawyer to help. The encouragement and the "permission" given by both the therapist and the mediator for me to express my feelings and concerns counteracted some of my deeply felt anxieties. I realized that by virtue of some of the things I had already said in this opening session, I had made what was probably my first formal admission that my marriage had failed.

I was worried about being held to binding arbitration if we were confronted with an impasse. I realized that although the mediator was going to be fair, he was not going to be on my side or on anyone's side for that matter. He was neutral, and when it came down to making real decisions, I was ultimately alone.

I left the first session feeling sad about having to face the reality that the marriage was ending. I still had a great deal of anxiety about this unknown process and how it would affect the rest of my life. I had trouble with the realization that I needed to become self-sufficient, and I was terrified of loneliness. Who would take care of me?

*Myles:* In between sessions, I felt very isolated and frustrated. I didn't know who to trust or who to ask for confirmation that I was doing the right thing. My own accountant and attorney told me that I was probably making a big mistake, that if I went to court I would never have to give as much to Karen as I had already agreed to during our voluntary separation. This warning was repeatedly drummed into me by my friends and associates. So I tried calling two lawyers that were recommended to me. They both thought I was making a poor decision by not using legal counsel, but they couldn't tell me what kind of financial settlement I would end up with in court. They did say that I would pay less than what I had already indicated I could provide—how much less they couldn't say. No one was giving any guarantees.

What it seemed to come down to was that I did not believe the possibility of saving a few dollars was worth the potential of a protracted legal battle. After all, what I saved in settlement payments might ultimately end up going to the lawyers. That alternative was not acceptable. I would rather give the difference to Karen and the children.

I tried to talk to a few friends and relatives, but they were no help. No one knew of anyone who had participated in a mediated divorce. The lack of confirmation of my decisions became very frustrating.

I had a fear of financial insecurity. This fear made it nearly impossible to make out a monthly budget for my needs. My lack of trust in Karen and the absence of the comfortable mediation setting made it difficult for me to feel I could walk in and divulge a list of all my property investments. Between sessions it was very difficult to keep faith in the process.

*Karen:*  I also could not find anyone with whom to share my thoughts and concerns about mediation. All my friends advised me that I was making a big mistake. The further away I was from the first session, the more the old fears and insecurities returned. I became more ambivalent and negative as each day passed.

I felt that the future was both emotionally and financially uncertain and, because of that uncertainty, frightening. I found working on the budget sheer torture, and trying to plan for future expenses for myself and the children terrifying. I called on a close friend for aid in working with the budgets and figures that made me so anxious. The stage was set for the next session.

CHAPTER 6

# How to Find A Mediator And What to Ask

**Y**our choice of a mediator should depend primarily on which issues are uppermost in your situation.

Some mediators prefer to work alone, some work in teams. A team can draw on the backgrounds of both members for additional insight. Some mediators like to work as a male-female team, because this may help the spouses avoid feeling that the mediator is favoring or identifying with the person of the same sex. Your comfort with the mediator is important to your confidence in the mediation. The mediator plays a crucial role in formulating an agreement that will affect you and your family for the rest of your life. It is essential, therefore, that you pick a mediator who has the training and experience to respond to your particular needs.

There are two classes of mediators—court-sponsored ones and private ones. There are nearly twenty states where court-sponsored mediation now exists, and there are pilot projects for mediation programs in many states. California, for example, has had conciliation agencies attached to its divorce courts for several years; in addition, the state has recently enacted a bill making mediation mandatory in all cases of contested child custody and visitation. Florida has a family conciliation unit in the circuit court of Fort Lauderdale.

Some of the places that have court-connected services funded by the state or county government are Alaska, Arizona, California, Colorado, Connecticut, Delaware, Florida, Hawaii, Illinois, Indiana (supported by client fees and divorce filing fees), Kentucky, Maine, Massachusetts, Michigan, Minnesota, Missouri, Montana, Nebraska, Ohio, Oklahoma, Oregon, Texas, Virginia, Washington, Wisconsin, Australia, and Canada.

## Finding a Mediator

To find a mediator, whether court-connected or private, a good place to begin is the local family court. Some courts offer free or low—cost services, but court-connected mediation services deal primarily with custody and visitation issues only, not with all divorce-related issues.

Believe it or not, the telephone number for the family court can be located in the white pages (or blue pages, if your directory has them) of the telephone book. Under the listings for local government, find the heading Courts. There should be a number for Court Information. The people who answer this number can be extremely helpful. It is also possible that in your particular locale, there is no Family Court. If this is the case, look under Domestic Relations Court, Juvenile Court, or Probate Court. They may be able to provide the right information or direct you to the best source.

Another possible avenue to take for locating the right information sources is to call the Family Mediation Association or the American Bar Association. Either will generally provide the names and numbers of mediators in your area. The Bar Association can also provide court numbers and information on services such as centers for community justice and divorce and stress clinics.

The American Arbitration Association can also provide help in finding mediators; however, information will not be given out over the telephone. You will be asked to make an appointment to come into the office for an interview. After the interview, they will suggest a mediator who they believe will suit your particular requirements.

In some states the conciliation courts are handling divorce mediation as it relates to custody and visitation arrangements. You can call the Conciliation Court to find out whether or not it handles marital mediation and whether it can provide a list of mediators. If it does not handle divorce cases, it usually has suggestions or information about which court in your area you need to contact.

There are also specialized mediation organizations that you can contact. Among them are:

- The Family Mediation Association (Bethesda, Maryland) (California)
- American Mediation Institute (Arizona)
- Family Mediation Network (Florida and California)
- Academy of Family Mediators (New York)
- Family Mediation Center (Ohio)
- Divorce Mediation Center (Charlotte, North Carolina)
- Family Mediation of Greater Washington (Arlington, Virginia)
- Center for Separation and Divorce Mediation, (Falls Church, Virginia)

There is a national listing for divorce mediators published by the Divorce Mediation Research Project in Denver, Colorado; it can be obtained by mail for approximately ten dollars.

It is also possible to find a private mediator by referral from other health professionals. Social workers affiliated with the local family court may know of some mediators. Sometimes the large, non-profit family welfare organizations can provide a list of mediators. Again, in the telephone book, check under Counseling, Family Counseling Centers, Social Services, Psychologists, Divorce Assistance, or Mediation Services. Calling local family service agencies can generally lead you to the names of people in your area who have had experience in mediation. Many therapists have at some time dealt with problems relating to divorce or custody and visitation. If they do not personally know of a mediator, they will usually try to give you some guidance toward finding one. One small but significant aid is that as of this year, mediation will be listed in the yellow pages of telephone directories under its own name—Mediation.

Mediation is still very new, and services are not always conveniently available. In smaller towns or cities without an office of The American Bar Association, a family mediation center, or a conciliation court, it may require a little digging to find the right information, but perserverance can go a long way.

## Key Questions

Once you have found a mediator, there are several key questions that need to be asked before you make a decision to proceed.

**Questions about the mediator's background**—A couple should be assertive in finding out about the background and credentials of the mediator. Find out what kind of training he has had. Be sure he has had special training in mediation. Don't be afraid to ask what the mediator's educational background is. Take the time to learn what kind of degrees he holds. Is he an attorney, a counselor, a social worker?

Different problems may require different specialties. It is important to find out whether the special expertise you think you may need can be provided by the mediator you're interviewing. Also, it helps if the mediator has a lot of experience and some knowledge of state divorce laws and of the tax issues involved. Does the mediator have a specialty? If you know that your biggest problem will be dealing with custody, you may want to locate a mediator who has extensive experience in dealing with the psychological or sociological effects of custody on children. If the mediator has limited expertise in a particular area (such as tax implications), check to see if he is willing to call on experts to provide assistance at the appropriate time. Most mediators have resource people with whom they regularly work.

**How are mediators trained?**—Generally, mediators will have at least a master's degree in one of the social sciences (psychology, sociology or counseling) or a law degree. They may also have work experience that is comparable to academic degrees.

What is of utmost importance is whether or not the mediator has had special training in conflict resolution or in family-divorce mediation. This training can be obtained from mediation associations, institutes, or private mediators who also conduct training sessions. The Family Mediation Association has initiated national certifiction for family/divorce mediators and offers both courses and a praticum leading to certification. Several universities such as the Catholic University and the University of Illinois have initiated two-year post-graduate programs in mediation. The American Arbitration Association trains mediators and arbitrators. The Family Conciliation Court Unit in Fort Lauderdale, Florida, supervises students in mediation internships. The Divorce Mediation Research Project of Denver has a printed national directory of organizations and individuals who do mediation training. This list can be purchased by mail.

It is important to note that currently no licensing requirements for mediators exist, so it falls to the couple to ask the mediator about his background, training, and experience before making any final decision.

## Questions about Cost

After you are satisfied with the mediator's credentials, the next important issue is money. *How much is this all going to cost?* The fee is usually based on cost per session or cost per hour. The hourly fee varies, but generally ranges between $35 and $60 per hour. If you are using a team of mediators, the cost may be slightly higher, depending on who is involved. You will also need to know how many sessions the mediator anticipates it will take to complete the agreement. There will generally be about five to seven sessions, with each session running between one and a half and two hours.

**How does the mediator want you to pay for the sessions?**— In most cases the couple will be asked to make a deposit to cover the first ten hours of mediation, plus an estimated amount to cover the cost of the additional charges for an advisory attorney. If there is any portion of the money that is not used, it will be returned to the clients if:

- the parties have reached a settlement;
- the parties have become reconciled or disabled; or
- the parties reach an impasse and have proceeded with arbitration.

**What additional costs will there be?**—Since an advisory attorney is required to provide legal advice, finalize the agreement, put all matters into appropriate legal form and, perhaps, file the final papers, her fee must be added to the estimate. This attorney may or may not attend a session. She seldom spends more than six hours on the case. The attorney will specify charges to which the participants must agree when they hire her. If the services of a tax consultant or psychologist are going to be used, these charges must also be included. Again, all charges will be itemized prior to the start of the sessions and will be stated on an hourly basis. After the mediation is completed, there will be a cost for a filing attorney who may or may not be the advisory attorney. There will also be court costs for filing for the divorce when the couple chooses to turn the separation into a legal divorce.

All of these charges may seem to imply a large expense, but compared to most adversary divorces and to the cost of two opposing attorneys, mediation is a bargain. Also, all charges are spelled out in advance and totals are estimated so that expenses don't mount up without the participants realizing what is happening.

**Who pays for mediation?**—The cost is split between the husband and wife. Responsibility for taking care of your part of the cost is a first step toward realizing you will be taking care of your expenses from now on. In the adversarial system, the woman often comes to an attorney with the belief that the husband is responsible for all the legal expenses. She assumed that she can retain a high priced bomber and her husband will foot the bill. This is not necessarily the way it happens. The man may be required to pay a percentage of the legal fees, but that amount will not necessarily cover even the retainer fee the attorney may require. The longer and messier the divorce, the greater the fees. They mount up faster than you think. Considerable sums of money, which might have been divided between the husband and wife, might now go to the attorney.

## Questions about the mediator's role

**Does the mediator give legal advice?**—No. The mediator is often not an attorney; however, even if he does happen to be an attorney, he is not permitted to be a counselor to either party. The mediator will generally make clear before the session begins that he has no legal authority and therefore cannot compel the parties to reach an agreement. The mediator's intention is not to judge either person or to force a position on them. The mediator will assist the couple only in arriving at a settlement; the advisory attorney will provide legal advice. The parties need to understand that they have the option to seek additional legal advice during mediation if they choose.

**What is the function of the mediator?**—The mediator has many different functions. Initially he sets the tone and agenda for the sessions. As the sessions begin, the mediator will serve as a "legitimizer." In this capacity he "encourages each party to recognize the other's right to disagree. He symbolizes the legitimacy of the issues and the potential for resolution of disagreement."[1]

The mediator also functions as an educator or trainer. He teaches the couple how to negotiate as the sessions progress. He also trains the couple in the application of problem-solving techniques, through the use of open-ended probing questions designed to stimulate their thinking. He helps open new lines of communication between the two people and gets them talking and listening to each other, and he helps clarify, define, and identify points of agreement. As he gradually trains the couple in the art of communication, he also serves as a "humanizer."

By developing both the listening and understanding skills of the couple, he can help them break down the stereotypes of each other that they have developed. This makes it possible for them to be more open to recognizing potential solutions.

Throughout all the sessions the mediator's role is to help keep a workable solution as the focus. He helps keep both parties aware of what is possible and impossible in their particular situation.

**Is the mediator impartial?**—In all aspects of his role, the mediator serves to aid in reaching a settlement. He is able to accomplish this by remaining objective and impartial. His allegiance cannot be to either party, but to the settlement. His only interest is that the parties arrive at a fair and workable agreement with which they are both satisfied.

The mediator remains absolutely impartial throughout the sessions. Actions that a mediator may take to ensure that the rules are being upheld may appear to one side to be favoring the other; however, as mediation progresses, it will be apparent that it was the process not a particular person that was being supported.

**How can I be sure that the mediator will remain impartial?**—You can be comfortable with the knowledge that an experienced mediator knows how to remain unbiased and impartial throughout a case. It is a critical condition of his position. With the proper training in negotiation skills and conflict resolution, and with extensive experience, the mediator will have learned to be a strong but fair manager of the process.

All of us have some biases, and it is possible for them to surface at times. Generally, the mediator will tell you this is happening should it occur. It you are very concerned about this possibility, you may choose to use a team of mediators as added protection against coalitions between participants.

**Does the mediator talk with me individually?**— According to the marital mediation rules, the parties involved are not to consult with either the mediator or the advisory attorney individually. All communication is done directly and always in the presence of both participants in the mediation process. This helps to avoid any fear of "a conspiracy."

There are some mediators, however, who do not agree with this approach; they prefer to hold separate sessions with each party to learn more about the individual's strengths and weaknesses. Some mediators feel that individual discussions allow each spouse to express what is on his mind, unhampered by the power role that he habitually plays in the relationship. Such sessions also give the mediator a chance to explore some underlying issues and to get a sense of what he may expect during the coming sessions. If either of these methods feels more comfortable for you, check with the mediator before beginning the sessions to learn whether he follows the structural rules or holds individual interviews. Each mediator has his own style.

In our case, although our mediator basically followed the structural rules, he occasionally made exceptions when he felt they were necessary. After one particularly emotional session, he requested a short meeting with one of us. The other was told about this in advance and asked it if would be all right. It was agreed on, and neither one of us felt that the mediator had shown any bias or partiality.

**Can I talk with the mediator between sessions?**—Those mediators who follow the rules of structural marital mediation will not permit private conversations with either party between sessions. Other mediators may be more open to private conversations and even encourage the individuals to call if they feel the need to do so. You will need to find out which method your mediator chooses to follow and with which you feel you will be more comfortable.

**If I talk to the mediator between sessions, is the information confidential?**—If your mediator is one who permits private conversations between sessions, then you can be certain the information you discuss will be confidential. The mediator, in order to facilitate the session, must have the trust of both parties involved. Any breach of confidence would erode the trust that is fundamental to the mediation process.

**What if the mediator does not feel the settlement reached is fair? What if anything, can he do?**—Before a settlement is signed, a couple may want an assurance from the mediator that their agreement is reasonable, complete, and maintainable. If this evaluation is requested, the mediator has a responsibility to provide it. When the final agreement has been reached, the mediator indicates whether he thinks it is fair by giving his concurrence. If a mediator is not in agreement with the settlement, he may note his non-concurrence. However, whether or not the mediator concurs will have no effect on the legality of the agreement.

This non-concurrence, however, is the most important form of intervention the mediator has. Psychologically, it carries a powerful message. Usually, if a mediator is displeased enough with an agreement to enter a non-concurrence opinion, then either both parties or the one the mediator believes is getting a bad deal will usually want to reevaluate the settlement and attempt to reach a more equitable solution. If they choose to retain the agreement as is and not reconsider, the mediator may choose to disassociate himself from the agreement, although the agreement still stands. This is a very rare occurrence. In addition, the mediator would hope that his non-concurrence would alert the court at the time of the divorce to evaluate the proposed settlement carefully before approving the final divorce decree.

**Can the mediator be asked to testify on behalf of or against either party if the case goes to court?**—No. As part of the rules of mediation, both the Family Mediation Association and the parties involved must agree that all communication that takes place during mediation will be privileged. That means that this information may not be used if the parties should decide to pursue a settlement in court.

**Are tape recordings of the sessions ever made?**—Most mediators tape-record their sessions. This is done only with the couple's approval. All information is confidential. These recordings are used only to clarify issues in case there is confusion and to help the mediator when it comes time to draft the memorandum. Either party can listen to the tapes by requesting to, but the tapes remain the property of the mediator.

**Does the mediator make decisions?**—The mediator does not make decisions for you. He provides information and guidance, but the actual decisions are made by the people who will have to live with them. The mediator serves as a catalyst to help you see alternatives. He assists in problem-solving and can help to redefine an issue in a way that makes it easier to reach a solution, but the solutions and decisions will not come from him. You must take the responsibility for them yourself.

**How do mediation, conciliation, and arbitration differ?**—Mediation involves the use of a neutral third party who helps guide the couple toward making their own decision. The mediator does not make any decisions on his own. He may stimulate discussions to help the couple look at as many options as possible, but responsibility for decisions rests entirely with the couple.

Conciliation involves a neutral third party who provides guidance for the couple. However, the conciliator can make recommendations and can bring up additional options that the couple may not have thought of previously. The conciliator points out the advantages and disadvantages of various options and may press the couple to agree on an option already available so as to avoid being stuck. To some degree, conciliation usurps the couple's role in the problem-solving process that precedes decision-making.

Arbitration also involves a neutral third party, but it differs from mediation and conciliation in that the arbitrator makes decisions for the couple. The arbitrator listens to both sides and then makes a decision that both parties are bound by previous agreement to uphold. Both parties compete with each other for a favorable decision. Usually there is no appeal from the arbitrator's decision, and it is enforceable by law in most states.

## Questions About the Sessions

**Where do sessions take place?**—Sessions usually take place in the mediator's office or home. If the mediator is an attorney, he may use a conference room, library, or private office. Many mediators prefer to hold the sessions in their home. This tends to provide a comfortable, relaxed, and informal atmosphere. Any room or office that is quiet and free from distractions and interruptions is a suitable environment for mediation. This kind of setting tends to reduce some of the tension and gives the mediation process a personal touch.

**How long are the sessions?**—The sessions generally last from one to two hours, depending on the issue being considered and on the mediator's preferred way of operating. Most structured mediation sessions are scheduled for two hours and are held once a week. It is possible, however, that the mediator may opt for a different schedule based on his sense of the optimum intervals between sessions and on difficulties of coordinating schedules. Some mediators prefer to stick to a fixed schedule; others are more flexible, allowing from one to five hours for a session. Some mediators feel that adhering to a rigid time limit would be too restrictive, especially during intense sessions, for which more time may be necessary.

**How many sessions will there be?**—Mediation tends to average about five two-hour sessions in addition to the initial orientation session. Usually, by the third session, substantive agreements have been reached. The fourth session may be spent with the advisory attorney. If there are any unresolved issues at the end of the third session, the couple and the mediator must decide whether to extend the sessions for four or more hours, or to declare an impasse on certain issues. Some mediators prefer to have more but shorter sessions, but each case is so different that it is difficult to pin down exactly how many are required to reach an agreement.

On the average, mediation will proceed far more rapidly than negotiation between adversarial attorneys, because after ten hours the mediator or either party may declare an impasse. On impasse, the parties, by their previously signed contract, must submit the unresolved issue(s) to arbitration. Thus a clear time limit is set. Arbitration is rarely needed.

**Can sessions exceed the allotted time if a matter of importance is still under discussion?**—This depends on the mediator's philosophy and how he chooses to handle the time issue. As with the previous question, those who follow structured mediation tend to stick more rigidly to prearranged schedules. They feel that people work more productively within known limits. Other mediators are more flexible and allow sessions to exceed their allotted time if necessary. Be sure to ask your mediator how he feels about this issue.

**Do the children participate in the sessions?**—The Family Mediation Association rules provide that children shall be entitled to participate in mediation sessions related to their interests. The mediator may suggest that an additional special session be held with the children present for working out visitation arrangements. This is a very helpful and highly recommended procedure; however, it is not essential. Should you not agree that it is useful in your particular situation, it will not be included in the mediation agenda.

**Does the mediator represent the children?**—In essence, the mediator represents only the process. He is not a spokesperson for either party or for the children. Sometimes children can be called in to express their opinions. Whether or not their participation is included, the mediator will work with the couple to create an agreement that provides the most benefit for the children.

**How does the mediator keep one person from dominating the session?**—The mediator exerts a quiet, almost imperceptible control over the sessions. By adhering to the mediation rules, he is able to maintain an equality between the two people. The rule that forbids one person from interrupting the other ensures that each person is given an equal chance to speak and be heard. No one is permitted to dominate a session or to use any tactics that prevent the other from being heard. If one person has been particularly long-winded on a particular topic, the other person is given an equal opportunity to respond without interruption.

Mediation teaches you to be responsible for yourself: not being dominated by your ex-spouse or not being fearful of speaking up is a first step toward adjustment to your new life. Since the agreement that will ultimately be reached is so personal and specific, it is to your advantage to work jointly and as equals to make the decisions on which it will be based. Learning to rely on your own strengths in these sessions will give you new capabilities that will help you avoid future domination, whether in marriage or other areas of your life.

**If I am feeling intimidated by my spouse during a session, how can I make that known to the mediator and how can I let my spouse know I won't tolerate it?**—When mediation begins, people are generally feeling very stressed and helpless. They may feel easily intimidated by their spouse. The mediator is trained to be aware of these emotional states. He will provide support and structure, and confidence in his own ability to handle the situation. Slowly he will build the confidence of the couple and provide them with evidence that they can handle their situation, no matter how difficult it may seem. As these strengths and abilities develop, it becomes easier to face a spouse as an equal and to indicate clearly that unacceptable or inappropriate remarks or innuendos will not be tolerated.

As mediation progresses, you will decrease your reliance on the mediator as your shield. As you perceive that your own strengths can prevent anyone from exerting control over you, you will not only have established equality in the mediation, but also have diminished the possibility of your being intimidated in the future.

## Questions about Mediation

**Is mediation for everyone?**—Though we believe very strongly in the process, we would be hard-pressed to state that mediation is for everyone. We do believe that the vast majority of people considering separation and divorce could benefit from mediation. There are, however, a few people who are poor candidates for taking the responsibility of negotiating their own agreement. These people are clearly identifiable:

- Those who are very ambivalent about the decision to divorce. These are couples where one or both are just not able to face the prospect of divorce. They will tend to argue over every detail and battle every step of the way. One or the other will use all kinds of techniques to prolong the relationship or sabotage divorce efforts.
- Couples whose fear of conflict or direct communication with their spouse is so strong that they just cannot envision themselves (or at least one of them cannot) negotiating with each other at all.
- Couples with such intense hostility and bitterness that the desire for revenge is still the primary goal. In these circumstances, a mediator would recommend therapy before beginning medition.
- Couples where one partner may have a history of psychological problems. If there has been spousal or child abuse, or other conditions that make trust and negotiating impossible, mediation is inappropriate.

**Is mediation appropriate for couples without children?**—The advantages of mediation apply to most couples with conflicts over how to end their marriage. Couples without children can use mediation as readily as those with children. Every couple has its own set of issues to negotiate. Children are not a prerequisite.

**Can homosexual couples use mediation?**—Whether the couple involved in breaking up a relationship is heterosexual or homosexual has no bearing on the relevance of mediation. A couple uses mediation to help them achieve a dissolution of their relationship—the nature of that relationship is not in question. Mediation can be very useful for homosexual couples in that it provides an avenue other than the adversarial system for handling a very personal situation.

**Does mediation always work?**—Unfortunately, mediation doesn't always work. The biggest stumbling block to successful mediation is the non-mutuality of the decision to divorce. Couples who are ambivalent about the decision to divorce will sabotage any efforts to reach agreements. If the partners are at different stages in their acceptance of the divorce, one person may make negotiating impossible. In this case, the person who feels he did not want this divorce will probably try to hold on to the other person or try to make them pay for the pain they have caused. This vindictive attitude will interfere with mediation.

These people should not have started mediation in the first place. They weren't ready. A mediator would recognize this sitution at the orientation session. He would discuss with the couple the fact that it only takes one person to get a divorce. Holding on by the unwilling party will not prevent the divorce from happening. If one or both people feel they need time to think about the situation or perhaps get some outside help, a temporary halt can be called to mediation until they both feel ready to proceed.

**What happens if we cannot agree?**—If mediation has been started and the structured rules have been signed, then an impasse on a particular issue triggers the need for arbitration. During arbitration, the right to decide is turned over to a neutral third party—an arbitrator. The arbitrator's decision is final and binding. She will hold a hearing and will reach a decision called an award. This decision will be incorporated into the settlement agreement. Arbitration is very rarely needed, because couples most often find ways to work things out rather than submit to binding decisions imposed by others.

**How can I be sure of full financial disclosure by my spouse?**—Marital mediation requires full disclosure by both parties of all financial information regarding income and financial holdings. This includes copies of income tax returns, personal financial statements, and financial statements from any business or professional corporations that either party owns or has any shares in. These are checked by the mediator. By comparing the items on the tax returns to those submitted on the accompanying lists, he can find out if any assets have been omitted from the financial statements. Also, a warranty is written into the agreement, in which both parties attest to the accuracy of their disclosures. When all marital property and individual needs have been identified, the parties can begin to work out an acceptable division, to be formalized in the agreement.

**What if all is not disclosed about the financial situation and I find out later?**—Whether one gets divorced via mediation or the adversary approach, it is possible for a person, who is willing to take the risk, to lie or fail to disclose some financial holdings. However, the consequences are severe if that action is discovered. If you find out that your spouse has not provided a complete financial disclosure, you can return to mediation to renegotiate the agreement using mediation or arbitration. If your spouse refuses to cooperate, you can always get an attorney or apply to the court of competent jurisdiction for modification of the agreement. The consequences of not providing full disclosure in either approach can be costly.

**Does mediation encourage divorce?**—Both by philosophy and by policy, mediation does not encourage divorce. Structural mediation is a method that is used once the decision to divorce has already been made by the couple. The clearer they are about that decision, the more smoothly the mediation process will work. Couples are often referred to mediation by therapists who have been working with that couple because of marital difficulties. It is only after the couple has decided that divorce is inevitable and that they wish to seek mediation—then and only then is the referral made.

**What is the result of mediation?**—The couple and the mediator arrive at a workable arrangement that the mediator writes up in everyday language. The advisory attorney provides legal advice, structures the agreement, and drafts it into a clearly worded, final legal separation agreement. The end result of mediation is a detailed separation agreement that is legally binding and will be accepted in court.

**How long does the separation agreement last?**—The separation agreement is a permanent legal agreement between the parties and will remain in force until the couple decides to seek a divorce. At that time, the separation agreement becomes a part of the final judgment and decree of divorce. Of course, it may be modified before the final decree. Having the document in hand, turns the actual divorce into an easy and mechanical procedure.

**Should we discuss the sessions with relatives and friends?**—Mediation rules stress that it is important not to discuss the sessions with outside persons. Realistically though, most people feel the need to discuss the sessions with their family or friends. It is far too important an issue in your life to keep to yourself. The caveat is that everyone will try to give you advice and opinions. Remember that no situation is exactly like yours, and you probably won't find many people who are familiar enough with mediation to give it a fair interpretation. People tend to make adversarial and counterproductive statements—"Be sure you get this...." "Don't give that...." If you can keep the comments and advice of others in perspective, talking to other people may help you clarify your own thinking.

**If we settle an issue and one person wants to reopen it, is that possible?**—When agreement has been reached on an issue, the mediator states the resolution and if both people understand and agree, the issue is closed. It cannot be reopened without the authorization of the mediator. This is to prevent issues from dragging on indefinitely. If the mediator feels that a mistake needs to be corrected or that new information has become available, he will permit an issue to be reopened.

**Once we are divorced, can we go back and reopen an issue?**—You can return to mediation to renegotiate any part of your agreement. You can also apply to a court of competent jurisdiction to modify support payments (up or down) if your circumstances have changed. Custodial arrangements too can be modified, but a court order is required to bring about a legal change in the arrangement. Most people who have reached a mediated settlement opt for a return to mediation before resorting to the courts.

**What happens if one person doesn't live up to the agreement?**—One of the positive aspects of a mediated settlement is that this very seldom happens. There is usually a commitment to a jointly prepared agreement. If it should happen, however, you can return to mediation and renegotiate the issue that is causing difficulty, or you can arbitrate, or you can go to court if all else fails.

**What if I disclose information in mediation but end up using the adversary system—can this information be used against me?**—All material in mediation is confidential and cannot be used as evidence. Mediators cannot be called as witnesses in litigation nor are they required to produce records, documents, or tapes of mediation sessions.

**What are the laws pertaining to property division in my particular state?**—When a marriage dissolves, all the marital property is put into a pool and divided up. Some states, like California, split the assets fifty-fifty. Others split them according to guidelines such as how long the marriage lasted and how much each partner contributed. A responsible mediator will have this knowledge and will make sure the couple has all the information they need. This knowledge will help give you an idea of what you might get if you leave the decision to the courts. It is important to remember, however, that in mediation it is the two parties involved who decide how to split all the property. Other guidelines need not apply.

**Do I need an attorney?**—The only attorney needed for the mediation process is the advisory attorney. She is used as an impartial advisor to both parties and drafts the memorandum of agreement into a legal document. This attorney will be picked by both parties, either on their own or from a list provided by the mediator. In addition, each person has the option to get independent legal counsel to review the agreement prior to signing.

**What if I'm interested in mediation and my spouse isn't?**—This is a difficult situation to handle on your own. If you contact a mediator, he can then call your spouse to present a detached viewpoint and discuss unemotionally the benefits of mediation. The mediator can also send you and your spouse information about mediation. Don't decide in advance that your spouse "will never agree to mediate." Let the mediator explain the process, then let your spouse decide for himself. You may also get help from friends who may have been through mediation. If you have been seeing a family therapist, she may be able to help too. In short, it helps to get professional assistance in presenting the benefits whenever possible.

In this chapter, we have briefly addressed what we consider to be many of the most important questions about mediation; however, they do not represent an exhaustive list. Many of these questions as well as others are discussed in greater detail in upcoming chapters.

## CHAPTER 7

# Custody and Visitation

## Our Mediation

For some people, custody can be a very traumatic and painful issue. There is so much ego involved that it is often difficult to separate facts from underlying questions of power and authority.

When we began our session on custody and visitation, we thought that custody was not going to be a difficult issue. We had already decided that Karen would retain custody, since the children were so young and were used to her being the one primarily responsible for their care. We agreed that it was in the children's best interest for Myles to have liberal visitation rights, so that he could be actively involved in their lives. Major decisions regarding the boys would be made jointly.

There were many pitfalls that we didn't foresee at the time. Fortunately, a lot of the skills we learned in negotiating our settlement enabled us to negotiate with each other further down the road to overcome those pitfalls. Questions about camp, birthday parties, extracurricular activities, just to mention a few, could have been occasions for unresolvable conflicts. In agreeing to consult each other on major decisions, we had indicated a respect for each other's opinions and feelings. This respect would help prepare us for our future dealings.

Thinking that because we had settled the big question of custody we would slide easily through visitation arrangements, we began to work out a visitation schedule. We discovered that, even though we thought we had this all worked out, we still had many unresolved issues to deal with.

Karen had devoted all her energies to the care of the children. It was difficult for her to accept their being out from under her control. She found the thought of Myles taking over "her role" both threatening and unbearable. She didn't know what she would do without her children as her constant focal point and responsibility. That sudden transition from total involvement with her children to "too much time alone" was difficult to comprehend and, at least initially, difficult to accept.

*Myles:* I had not come to terms with the guilt I was experiencing about having moved away from my children, and I was very insecure about my relationship with them. I pressed for more and more time with them to prove that I was a good father. The harder I fought for more time, the more Karen resisted, and the more she began to panic. Neither of us was facing reality. In our individual ways, we were struggling to maintain roles that no longer had any meaning. Separation was now a reality, but neither of us was yet willing to accept the finality of that situation.

*Karen:* We had been married for thirteen years. It isn't easy to just stop thinking in terms of a whole family unit. I still kept setting the table for four—and buying four tickets at a movie theater window. Being a wife and mother is not a nine-to-five job that I could suddenly stop doing. Without those well-defined roles, I felt I no longer had an identity. The more the children would be away from me, the more frightened I became about the lack of purpose and direction to my life. The children were my source of self-definition. They were my family, my reason to keep going—in short, my life.

*Myles:* My role as a father needed to be redefined, while she wanted her role reinforced. How do you learn to be a part-time parent? We were each fighting primarily for our own survival. Our haphazard agreement of dividing up days and times for visitation was just another weapon we used in our dominant/submissive relationship.

*Karen:* In our marriage, we had almost never maintained a relationship as two equals. One of us was always up and the other down. If things were going well for Myles, I would fear his not needing me, and play a submissive, dependent, and needy role. If his problems at work made him feel insecure or depressed, I would be the strong one and pull him back up again. We never really shared equally in major decisions. I always deferred to Myles and allowed him to be the boss. Vying for time with the children was just another chance for us to fall into old patterns of relating or not relating. I was experiencing such fear that he would take over again that I wasn't sure I could give an inch without it turning into a mile.

## The Visitation Schedule

We had not been consciously aware that our informal visitation schedule was a tool we could use to get back at the other. If we were "busy," we could use that as an excuse for arranging that the children should visit the other spouse. Who had what plans could be dangled in front of the other as an indication of who had made the quickest adjustment or had the better social life. The fact that the children were never sure when they would be where really didn't seem as important as our volleying for power. Karen, in particular, was resistant to setting up a rigid schedule because it meant facing the fact that the family truly was no longer a unit. The restructuring that was taking place was going to be permanent. It had seemed to Karen that the informal bargaining we had been going through about when Myles would spend time with the children was just a juggling act to be done until Myles returned home.

The mediator, realizing that we had these unresolved problems, began by encouraging us to express our feelings and fears about custody. He suggested that we openly discuss what we could and could not tolerate regarding time with the children. Slowly, we worked out a way to reach a solution with which we could both be comfortable. This represented our first major accomplishment.

Because of the situation and our experience so far, we agreed that we would approach change gradually. Myles's time with the boys would increase slowly, beginning with one afternoon and evening every other weekend, and finally expanding to the entire weekend every other week. This approach would allow both Karen and the children time to adjust to the changes. The children could also deal with the separation from Karen in a gradual way.

To formalize this new arrangement, the mediator insisted that we write down the schedule on a large calendar. Even with all our newly acquired understanding, we both resisted at first. Putting the agreement on paper seemed to be a major stumbling block. It represented visible proof of the reality of the separation, and that was difficult to face. It actually took two sessions to complete the calendar. When we had finally completed it, we were physically and emotionally exhausted.

We had gotten past the surface issues and were actually beginning to face the issue of the divorce. The mere fact that we were able to complete a task together was a surprise. We had focused on the issues and not on attacking each other. This realization gave us hope that we could create a viable agreement. At this point, we were even able to discuss Myles's desire to be with the children during the week. At first a conflict arose over what arrangements could be made, and what activities were reasonable for school nights.

The question of activities for school nights doesn't appear tremendously important, looking back, but almost any issue, big or small, in this situation seemed insurmountable. Karen had strong feelings that movies and late activities were inappropriate for school nights. She felt that it caused disruption in the children's routine, leaving them tired, irritable, and sometimes uncontrollable the following day. The movies were fun for Myles and the boys, but Karen would have to deal with the consequences. Myles resisted being "told" what he could and could not do, and felt that he was as capable of making those decisions as Karen. Karen had a difficult time accepting the fact that Myles would be in control during those evenings and that it was not up to her to judge how he spent his time when he was with the children.

The issue was resolved when we finally began to listen to each other. We set up a schedule with Myles spending time with the children at Karen's house during the school year. Myles would be responsible for maintaining the regular school night routine, giving the children dinner, helping with their homework, and putting them to bed. Karen would use this time for herself, away from home. During school vacations, Myles would take the children to his house, the movies, or elsewhere, since schedules were then more flexible. This "win-win" solution helped Myles feel more directly involved in the children's daily routine, while also providing some relief for Karen from the daily demands of raising the children.

At this time the mediator asked if we would like to have the children attend the next session. He felt it would help to clarify things for them and give them an opportunity to express their thoughts and feelings. We felt that their participation would cause them too much additional stress. They were not yet in a position to separate what was going on from feeling in some way responsible. We felt that we were taking their welfare and needs into consideration and that, at four and six, they were too young to be placed in the middle while their lives were being tossed around. The mediator used the occasion of our agreement on this issue to point out our areas of cooperation and our resolution of what had earlier seemed insurmountable issues. He indicated that we had covered a lot of ground.

*Karen:* I felt that my greatest contribution over the preceding thirteen years was having been a "good" and supportive wife, and having and raising my children. I had given my family as much of me as I could possibly give, and I was proud of having made that commitment and lived up to it.

Now that Myles had left, I was holding on to the children primarily because I had invested so much of myself in their nurturing. It seemed to me that Myles had gotten everything he wanted—his freedom, his new life, his secure financial position—and now he wanted to take the children too. I jealously guarded my relationship with the children. Now more than ever I felt they were all I had. I resented giving up any time with them. For the six years since the oldest was born, I had not worked outside of the house. Two babies made that impossible. By this time I had little or no independence and no sense of myself as a person of substance. I felt that my job had been raising my children. Now I needed them as a crutch while I hobbled around looking to make something of my shattered life. Now I needed to grow up, and I needed their help. My own development had suffered, and now I needed a crash course in self-development. I didn't feel useful, needed, and certainly not rewarded except in terms of the children.

Mediation provided a structure to begin rebuilding my life. The first step was the taking on of new responsibilities—responsibilities for making my own decisions, for arguing my own case. Taking on these new responsibilities and the independence that went along with it, even in small increments, made it possible for me to accept the changes gracefully.

At first I resisted the formalizations, the structuring of a visitation schedule. It meant to me that I was involved in a situation that was for real. That reality wasn't pleasant. This was no rehearsal. This was the real thing. What was decided now would in a most significant way guide the rest of my life. If I didn't participate, it was going to be arranged for me. That realization had a major impact on my involvement. The emotional realities were beginning to take shape for perhaps the first time. Myles, as the father of my children, was critical to their emotional well-being. Whether I liked it or not, he was an equal partner in their parenting. The children weren't mine or his. They were two separate individuals who needed both a mother and a father. The fact that our marriage was over didn't mean they should be denied the opportunity to have the best of both parents. I needed to grow up quickly. I needed to be willing to share the children with their father.

*Myles:* I was living through my own version of hell. I was dealing with guilt and pain over the effects of the divorce on the children. Not being involved in the daily lives of the children was a hard thing to accept. The calender represented finality to me. I would have to miss daily activities that the children were involved in; I would not be party to their everyday thoughts.

Mediation helped to give me more freedom to take an active role in the children's lives while still maintaining a structure. It helped me feel that I was a capable parent who would be consulted and involved in major events in the children's lives. I would not be left feeling as though my only role was paying for things in which I had little or no participation.

These little but important steps in gaining independence helped to generate self-confidence for both of us, and self-confidence was the key to negotiating the remainder of the settlement.

CHAPTER 8

# Negotiation
# Skills

*Conflict*— a contest, a fighting or struggling for mastery; a striving to oppose or overcome active opposition; a contention, controversy, strife.

*Divorce*—a dissolution of bonds of matrimony; separation of a husband and wife by judicial sentence; most divorces represent or are synonymous with conflict.

*Negotiation*—a process for resolving conflict and for minimizing causes of conflict in the future.

## Conflict

Conflict itself is neither good nor bad. Yet there is a critical differentiation to be made between destructive and constructive conflict. A conflict is said to be construtive or have productive consequences "if the participants all are satisfied with their outcomes and feel that they have gained as a result of the conflict." A conflict has destructive consequence "if its participants are dissatisified with the outcomes and feel they have lost as result of the conflict..."[1] The goal is not how to eliminate or prevent conflict, but how to make it productive.

Conflict has in fact many positive functions. Through conflict, solutions to a problem can be arrived at. Conflict is a stimulant to personal awareness, leading to change and growth. It forces you to analyze your position in order to present it more thoroughly. By pushing you to examine your patterns of thought and behavior, it encourages you to alter and revitalize your old ways of doing things and provides the opportunity to come up with new ways. Conflict can be a way of testing yourself and establishing your identity.

The adversary system fosters destructive conflict, which is characterized by a tendency to escalate. This often becomes so bitter that the original causes become irrelevant and may even be forgotten. It also tends to have negative long-term effects. In destructive conflict, both parties are dissatisfied with the outcome and tend not to let go of the issues. Each party is preoccupied with striving for control and dominance.

## Three Strategies of Conflict Resolution

The resolution of conflict can be achieved by three different strategies: the "lose-lose," the "win-lose," and the "win-win" strategies.

In the *lose-lose strategy* everyone loses. Everyone is dissatisfied with the results, feels bitter, and has no sense of commitment to the decisions. Both sides generally feel that they have compromised too much or that they have given up too much. They have gotten a raw deal, been cheated in some way, or have been made a fool of by their opponent. Neither side feels any sense of achievement or pride in the result.

The *win-lose strategy* is a competitive approach. It generally results when one person exerts power over the other. Enhancing one's own power and minimizing the other's becomes a prime objective. Winning is the goal. Anything that it takes to succeed is acceptable. The effects on the other party are of little or no concern. One person must by definition be the loser. That person is left feeling defeated, hostile, bitter. The loser then tends to seek ways to retaliate, and the desire for revenge becomes uppermost. The loser experiences frustration, is uncooperative, and may attempt to subvert the final decision. Implementing the resolution is difficult. Further conflict is likely as hostility builds, and one side or the other begins to engage in outrageous behavior based on the need for retaliation.

The *win-win strategy* is based on a cooperative or collaborative approach. Working in a problem solving mode, common goals are examined and alternatives are analyzed. Both sides feel satisfied with the results, which have been worked out jointly. Decisions are more likely to be upheld, and implementation of the solutions is generally without major difficulty, and often even easy. Since the conflict is resolved in a satisfactory way for both parties, there is less likelihood that there will be conflict in the future. A cooperative relationship has been established that will be a strong factor in future negotiations.

Mediation emphasizes the win-win method of conflict resolution. Each person has a sense of having gained while realizing that the other person also has to make gains. The adversary system, on the other hand, is generally a win-lose, and sometimes a lose-lose, system.

## How Mediation Helps Identify and Resolve Conflict

A primary objective of mediation is to help the two people involved identify and concentrate on the real issues of conflict. The mediator helps the two people confront each other in a productive way, focusing on issues, not emotions, so that they can cooperate to solve their problems. The mediator can regulate the degree of tension between the two people, and relieve their anxiety over possible blowups and tantrums when hot issues are discussed. She can also sequence the discussion from less to more controversial issues. She checks to see that both sides of each issue are expressed. She facilitates communication between spouses, checking to see that both parties listen to each other. She develops feedback mechanisms for verifying that each side has been accurately heard. The mediator keeps the two parties negotiating fairly.

## Mediation Creates a Framework for Negotiation

Negotiation is a method of getting what you want from others, based on give and take. The mediator in his neutral role recognizes the legitimacy of both sides and helps establish a framework within which a win-win solution can be achieved.

The mediator facilitates negotiations by seeing that the rules are followed. Of particular importance is the rule that requires each party to speak directly to the other and not to interrupt. The mediator's signing his approval of the settlement helps make the negotiators feel their settlement is fair, and his reactions can have a significant effect on how the settlement is viewed.

## Negotiating Techniques

Negotiating techniques are not a great mystery. The initial objective of negotiation is to make yourself heard. The mediator can assist by listening to each person and by helping the participants to clarify their views and attitudes. You won't have to scream or use noise makers to be heard. The stronger your feelings, the more likely it is that there will be nothing that you agree with the other person about.

To help make negotiation possible, it is necessary to remove as many barriers as possible. Therefore, don't do a lot of blaming. This usually causes the other person to get very defensive, to tune out what you are saying, and to begin to look for opportunities to retaliate. Try to focus on the issues without attacking or blaming the other person.

Look for opportunities to get the other person involved in determining the outcome. Give him a stake in the results so that he feels a commitment to the negotiating process. Generally, if people feel a project is theirs, they will work harder to achieve it.

If you are actively listening and making comments, asking questions that clearly indicate you are listening, a pattern will be established that will encourage the other person to do likewise. Listening requires work. If you want to be heard, you must be willing to listen.

Be specific! Jargon and wild ramblings are usually ignored. They are viewed as covers for the facts. People tend to stop actively listening when discussions become ambiguous and full of generalities.

These simple techniques are important prerequisites for negotiation. Making yourself heard and at the same time being able to listen are skills that can be learned. Don't panic. You too can be heard, even if you aren't capable of speaking out for yourself, even if you feel that talking to your spouse is a veritable impossibility. Don't give up—in mediation you are given a protective environment in which to be heard. You probably will find that being heard and trusted as an equal is a very enjoyable experience.

## Communication Skills

Communication is a skill that can be learned. Communication means not only being understood, but also seeking to understand. Speaking, in and of itself, is not communicating. Communicating is an active process of giving out and taking in information. "Without communication there can be no negotiation. Negotiation is a process of communicating back and forth for the purpose of reaching a joint decision."[2]

The only way to encourage communication is by being an active listener. Listening should not be confused with hearing. Hearing is simply the physical act, which only requires that you keep quiet enough while someone else speaks. Listening requires a conscious effort to understand and absorb what you hear. Active listening involves understanding what is being said in terms of both content and feeling. Active listening builds rapport with the speaker, shows that you understand and care, and generates a feeling of cooperation that further encourages dialogue. Being an active participant in the communication process involves listening with understanding. It means listening not only to what is said but also to what isn't being said. Omissions and evasions may be important clues to issues the other person wants to sweep under the rug.

**What To Watch For**—Watch out for generalities that may be used to avoid details and create a smokescreen around real issues. Listen for clues that double messages are being sent. Watch for contradictions between what she says and how she behaves. Look for discrepancies between statements and reality. Watch for evasive measures taken to skirt points of contention. Listen for Freudian slips that may reveal hidden meanings or intent. Watch for nonverbal clues that may indicate extreme anxiety or discomfort with statements being made. Is her body position relaxed, or is tension beginning to show? Arm crossing, thumb twiddling, eyebrow raising, hair twirling, fiddling with keys, or shredding tissues are some nonverbal clues to be noticed. Look for eye contact or lack of it. Does the other person look directly at you when he speaks? Does he avoid facing you? Be aware of head nodding. Affirmative or negative head nods indicate active listening on the other person's part. Notice the facial expressions of the other person. Lack of expression may indicate lack of interest. Listen for "I see-'s" or other verbal indicators that the other person is paying attention.

Listen carefully and ask for confirmation of points that you find unclear. Have the other party explain exactly what they mean. Repeat statements that the other person has made to be sure you know that what they said and what you heard were the same. "Did you say that…?" "When you said…your meaning was unclear…" If statements are ambiguous, then request clarification.

Notice how much time you spend talking instead of listening. There should be a balance between the two. When you are listening, try to limit the expression of your views. If you find that you are doing too much talking and dominating the discussion, stop and listen for awhile. If you are really listening, you will begin to distinguish facts from opinions. Both are valid, but one is no substitute for the other. Ask for sources if the other person is making claims that you feel need verification. Try not to hear only what you expect the other person to say. Be open to the possibility of change. Listen for positive statements that may be the basis for future points of agreement.

**Blocks to communication**—As part of all negotiating efforts, you must remain aware of some blocks to communication that can be used by the other participant. You should notice when he

- Attempts to attack or demolish everything you say.
- Implies that he knows something, but isn't telling.
- Paints an idealized picture of himself, covering up all weaknesses.
- Avoids talking at all, or avoids responding.
- Constantly attempts to change the subject.
- Ignores certain themes or issues.
- Attempts to put himself down, to get others to feel sorry for him.
- Acts helpless, dependent, or stupid as part of a strategy to win.
- Fails to listen actively to discussions, causing constant need for repetitions.

## Negotiating Pitfalls.

There are some very specific actions to avoid when negotiating. One major problem is that sometimes the two people involved do not talk directly to each other. They speak to the mediator and attempt to show off how wonderful they are, how generous, and how sacrificing. Try not to use jargon the other person can't understand. Don't try to impress the mediator or the other person with your superiority. Don't concentrate so hard on what you are going to say next that you stop listening.

Avoid the use of ultimatums. They generally put people on the defensive and set up a win-lose situation. Backing a person into a corner with either/or statements generally causes her to come out fighting. Opt for a softer approach.

Be wary of the soft sell or the begging and pleading approach by the other person. These techniques are meant to play on your guilt and are manipulative. They deflect you from your true feelings about a given issue. Don't fall prey to arguments that play on your emotions. Tears and suicidal threats are not appropriate negotiating tools. Don't be moved to give in out of guilt or the desire just to get things over with.

The solutions you reach now will affect your life for a long time to come. Try to avoid hanging onto an untenable position just for the sake of argument. Know where your limits are and stick to them, but remain ready to negotiate. If you can define the cause of conflict and analyze it in terms of what it means to each side, you can let go of the notion that your ego is on the line. Attempting to listen with empathy to the other side may help you shift your focus from attacking to achieving a solution.

Come to a session fully prepared for the issues to be discussed. If you are not prepared, and the other person has done her homework, you may well be at a disadvantage in the negotiation that follows. Lack of preparation may leave you without a proper set of alternatives from which to bargain. Being knowledgeable about the issues under discussion will help you feel more confident and less vulnerable.

It also helps if both parties are properly rested for the session. Being physically or emotionally exhausted can lead to difficult situations and unreasonable positions. If other problems are more pressing and demand attention, it may not be the best time to hold a session. Timing is an important factor in negotiations.

Confidence during negotiation sessions is important. If you think you have no power, you never will. Power is perceived. Don't allow veiled threats by the other person to make you feel vulnerable and powerless. We often give people power over us when in reality they have none. Many women tend to give men power over them, just by virtue of the fact that they are male. We may see older or wealthier or more educated people as having power over us, but much of this power is perceived rather than actual.

Don't attack the person, attack the problem. Try to keep from doing a lot of fault finding. There should be a balanced give and take— conciliation mixed with assertiveness. Neither a mouse nor an ostrich can be a successful negotiator.

## Successful Negotiating Techniques

There are several important ways to improve communication skills, and hence negotiation skills. Uppermost is the willingness to understand the ideas and attitudes from the other person's point of view. To try to sense how she is seeing the issues from her frame of reference is an important step in the process. To listen actively, without evaluating each statement from your perspective is not always easy, but it is necessary. Demonstrating an understanding of the other person's side helps foster a collaborative approach.

Establish a pattern of honesty and trust. Express your feelings about the other person's honesty and your faith in his intentions. Show concern for the other person's feeling, fears, needs. Look for opportunities to reach shared solutions. Pool ideas, find mutually beneficial outcomes. Find points that you can agree on and work from there. Make your points and present your ideas in nonthreatening ways. Direct your energies toward attacking the problem—not each other.

Know your position. Be prepared with the information you need and the reasons for your requests and denials. Be aware of the limitations that exist within your situation. What are the resources, restrictions, boundaries within which you are working? Have your priorities set, and have a plan formulated so that you can respond to new ideas. Know your bottom line on issues that are essential to you.

Work to narrow the differences between yourself and the other person. As the gap decreases, solutions become more possible. Try to be neither too adaptive nor too assertive. Maintain a sense of equality with the other person. This approach wll help facilitate an equitable solution to the problems. Equal involvement in the process will facilitate equal commitment to its implementation.

Use silence in the discussions when it is constructive. It can be a powerful tool. It may temporarily be uncomfortable, but don't start talking just to fill a void. Let the other person take responsibility for continuing the discussion when that is appropriate. You may obtain useful information. Silence by the other person may mean that she is thinking about ideas previously discussed, that she is analyzing new information, or perhaps that she is trying to shift the balance of power.

Listen patiently to the other person even if you do not agree or feel his point is relevant. Try not to get too emotional over specific statements. And try to understand first and evaluate later.

A useful technique is to summarize or paraphrase what has happened prior to taking action or making a decision. This ensures that both you and the other person have understood the other's position. It removes the possibility of later disagreement about what was agreed to by both parties.

Remember that it is your life that is being planned. You have the capacity to be instrumental in its direction. Have confidence in your ability to stand up for yourself. You can do it! No one has more interest in the decisions than you. Take responsibility for creating the framework on which you must build. The net result will be to your advantage. You will find that going forward from the mediation sessions is considerably easier than you ever imagined. A sense of control and direction, and positive expectations for the future will be the legacy you have earned.

CHAPTER 9

# General Financial Disclosure

## Our Mediation

**A**s we indicated in an earlier chapter, the problems that we had with custody and visitation surprised us to some degree. The discussions brought out some unresolved issues that we were not conscious of and, as a result, had not anticipated. Those issues related to whether or not each of us had the strength to face reality. Myles had to face the consequences of breaking up our home, of wanting the divorce in the first place, and of having to leave and no longer be with his children on a daily basis. Karen had to face the reality that her world of dependency was ending and that a need for independence had been thrust on her. We were steadily moving toward the reality of the divorce.

At least we had started. We had gotten through several significant issues. We had agreed on several steps. We had by this time begun to develop confidence in our mediator and the mediation process and, because of this, in our ability to deal with the issues. It was the mediator who had told us that trust and confidence were areas where we had problems, but until this point we had been unable to acknowledge that. Now we could see that was obviously correct. We both started to feel comfortable with him as an advisor, consultant, supporter.... We both felt he was competent, logical, and fair. We began to believe that mediation could actually work. The roller-coaster existence that we had been living was finally beginning to slow down.

By dealing with the areas of least contention first, we had assured ourselves that something would get accomplished. We both felt that trying to deal with finances first in our case would have been a mistake. We probably would have ended up in court as a result. The cold truth was finally beginning to set in.

By the time we had arrived at this point, we had both invested time and energy in the mediation, and we had seen some positive results come out of it. Because of this, we were more prepared to deal with the rougher topics. The impulse to leave that we both had felt at different times had lessened somewhat. We were now able to control our feelings of anger and mistrust enough to keep on trying to move ahead.

The financial issues were going to be a much more intense problem than anything we had to deal with concerning the children. We were in basic agreement about how to handle custody and visitation; we were not at all in agreement, however, about how we were going to deal with finances. In addition to feelings developed during our marriage, we both came from backgrounds that left us with feelings of insecurity when it came to financial matters. The reality, especially for Karen, of us each living independently with only one real source of income supporting two households was very frightening.

*Karen:* I had had few advantages during my earlier years. But by the time we started mediation, although Myles and I were far from high society, we were certainly living comfortably. I felt I deserved a share of the life we had built together, not just because I was married to Myles but because I had played a significant role in getting us to that point. I had supported the family during Myles's training, and I had played an active role in helping to get us through the early years when things were hard. I provided the financial support for us during the last two years of podiatry school and during the first year that Myles was a resident. The first few years of practice had also been a struggle, and I frequently helped out in the office to keep things going. In later years when someone got sick or a problem arose with the staff, I helped out. I also helped Myles with his writing throughout his schooling and as his reputation grew.

I had played an important personal and financial role in building our future, and I wasn't going to see all this work go unnoticed or unrewarded. I, too, wanted to reap some of the benefits of the years of working, planning, and struggling together.

For the previous six years, I had been home taking care of the children. I felt that I had sacrificed career opportunities and had been out of the job market long enough to make it difficult to return immediately. I had become financially dependent on Myles. I had no relatives to rely on and no other immediate source of income. Besides, even if I were to go out and work or begin a new career at this time, I knew that my earning potential was far less than Myles's. He had his profession, his income, and his investments, and I strongly believed a piece of that potential was rightfully mine.

We had suffered through the difficult years together and now, just as things were beginning to look good financially, Myles wanted a divorce. The threat of financial insecurity again after what I had been through almost all of my life was very terrifying to me and unjust. The great anxiety I felt translated itself into bitterness and resentment toward Myles.

*Myles:* My family, at least through my teenage years, had been financially secure. As a child I was somewhat spoiled and certainly had gotten used to having more than enough money. However, my family subsequently went through a sustained period of monetary crisis, and most of the financial security disappeared. This left me very insecure about making and saving money. I had expressed these feelings to Karen while we were together, and she was well aware of them. As a result, we had lived very frugally, even after I had started to make a decent living. We lived well below our means, saving as much as possible so as not to be left in the same position my parents were in when things went bad.

I really felt I couldn't cope with the financial pressures imposed by a divorce settlement. I was afraid that Karen would try and take me to the cleaners. I had heard about such nightmares from other people. I knew how upset she was with me. I was afraid there would not be enough left for me to have a life of my own if Karen were given a large piece of the pie.

## Emotional Baggage

Myles was not a very trusting person. Karen really had nothing to hide with respect to the financial disclosure required by the next mediation session. It was Myles who knew what they had, and he was still afraid that Karen would try to "bilk" him out of "his" money. As intelligent as Karen was, she had made no effort to be aware of their financial worth. She had always left money matters to Myles and, foolishly perhaps, had felt that it was not important for her to know the details of their financial situation. He knew he would have to disclose this information, because she would eventually find out. If she chose to go to court, all of the facts would come out. He was worried about whether or not in this case he could trust the mediator, the mediation process, and Karen to come up with a reasonable financial settlement.

Besides being mistrustful, Myles was angry. Some of this anger was at himself for being in this predicament and for having to be told what he should do with "his" money. After all, he had struggled to get where he was. He felt he deserved something to show for it, with or without Karen. He could not accept the fact that this money was also Karen's. She too had worked hard, had struggled. She too deserved something to show for it—with or without Myles. Without her work he wouldn't be where he was.

It was also hard for Myles to accept the idea that there were major parts of his children's lives that he would not be involved with, yet was expected to pay for. This was one of those harsh realities of divorce that must be dealt with, and he wasn't dealing with it yet. It left him very angry and anxious. His back was against the wall. There was just so much he could be expected to handle and that would be it. What "it" was, certainly was not defined.

This was the emotional baggage with which Karen and Myles approached the mediation session on financial disclosure and support.

## Documenting Finances

The way this session is handled is important. Each person is supposed to document in detail his monthly expenses as well as his future financial goals and needs, taking into consideration all future possibilities barring a major disaster. We had been given very detailed financial forms to complete. Everything was covered—savings, vacations, clothes, food, housing, health, insurance, special expenses, and everything else you could think of. First we had to deal with what we had had to live on up to now, and then what we believed we would need in the future. After all this was furnished, we would go over the financial disclosures to see what we actually had. This is another way of demonstrating the harsh reality of what divorce does to a couple—you want or believe you need a, b, c, and d, and so does your spouse; but nobody can have it all.

When we arrived at the session, the mediator asked whether we had worked out our financial forms. Karen said that she had. Myles, avoided answering the question, but finally let them both know that he hadn't done much work on it at all. It soon became evident as he floundered that he wasn't able to deal with what was happening. The realization of this contributed to his anxiety, and made him upset with himself. As he had always done, he turned his frustration with himself into anger at Karen. The only place to start, if they were going to continue, was with Karen's figures.

**Karen's Budget**—Karen proceeded to list her monthly budgetary needs, which came to more than what Myles was already giving her during the separation. This had an immediate effect on Myles. He was getting angrier and angrier as she continued; he was having trouble controlling himself. Some of his original anxieties about why he was there in the first place began to surface. Also, he felt angry at Karen because he wanted to be fair and to take care of her and the children, but he didn't want anyone to take advantage of him. He really couldn't see that he could afford to pay much more. He hoped that he could convince her of this.

One of the rules of mediation is that each side gets its turn on each issue. Thus, Karen was entitled to say all she had to about the monthly budget. Then Myles would have a chance to express his feelings. However, he found it very difficult to listen to her talk about this, and she went on and on, he started to fidget, and make faces and snide remarks. The mediator kept reassuring him that he would have his turn, reiterating to both Karen and Myles that he was not on anyone's side. He added that just because Karen wanted such and such didn't mean that she would get it.

Myles tried to remain calm. He recalls being thankful he had opted not to go to court—he would never have been able to sit still and listen. He resented not being in control of every situation, and he reacted with anger when he was not in control. He also realized Karen was finally learning to express herself, and that even though he would have equal time to respond, he could no longer dominate her as he had in the confines of their home throughout their marriage.

Myles finally lost control. He stood up, said it wasn't fair, that no court would ever force such a settlement on him. No one could ever force him to give her even as much as he was now paying. Besides,

Myles went on, if he were forced to give her all that, he would never have anything for himself. There would be no sense in working. He might as well just quit. They could all starve. Myles felt that Karen's supposed needs were extreme, that she was just trying to take advantage of him. He threatened to leave if this direction was to continue.

The mediator said that Myles ought to think about his options before he turned to the courts. Going to court is no picnic—you relinquish a great deal of control. He would not be allowed to express himself as he could here. Besides, he added, Karen's expressed needs would have to be evaluated carefully. Myles's needs still had to be heard. And everyone's needs had to be matched with available and projected resources. He suggested that Myles sit down so Karen could finish, and things could go on from there. He reiterated that one of the main purposes of this session was for both Myles and Karen to have an opportunity to describe their needs and to start to realize that their life-styles would have to change, no matter what happened. He asked Myles to listen to what Karen was saying so that he could respond to what she had said. Myles would soon have his turn. He stressed that any agreement would have to be worked out between the two of us, and suggested that in the meantime we both listen to each other and maintain control.

This exchange relieved some of the tension. Myles realized that they had come this far and that the alternatives were still not attractive. He was already here for this session, but didn't have to come back next week. He could call the whole thing off at any time, so he decided to sit down once again and allow the session to proceed.

Myles was concerned that Karen was purposely painting a picture of a poor helpless woman forced to care for two children with no independent source of income. He felt she was trying to gain everyone's sympathy so that he would be forced to give in to whatever she wanted. He had heard her story before—that it was a man's world, his potential was unlimited, he had all the advantages and she had made the sacrifices, that they were by no means in equal positions.

He also realized that he had not worked out his own needs. He figured from the looks of her budget, that Karen was getting outside advice. She also made it a practice to take notes whenever the mediator or Myles would say anything. This unnerved him, and he was certain she had an outside lawyer assisting her.

**Myles' Budget**—Myles stood up again, said he had had it and that he was leaving. Somehow the mediator calmed him down once again and suggested they begin going over his needs. Painstakingly, the mediator helped him fill out his monthly budget. He provided guidance and support, making the task less overwhelming. Myles began to realize that the mediator was in fact trying to be fair to both sides.

The figures for both Karen and Myles were written on a large piece of paper mounted on an easel. When this task was completed, the mediator had both of us copy what we each had listed. He explained that both of us had been unrealistic. Our expectations for continuing our existing life-style were not possible. We were to meet again in two weeks. During the intervening time, we were to try to talk to and listen to each other concerning these budgets. We were asked to think about the needs of the other so that a finite amount of money could be divided in the fairest possible way. Also by the next session, Myles was to provide full financial disclosure. Karen was to think more about actual needs versus wants, and to try to distinguish between them. We should both try to work on a give-and-take framework and push toward an agreement that would be solidified at the next session.

The instructions presented each of us with something to deal with before the next session. While the prospect of continuing upset each of us for opposite reasons, we realized this was a fair process. No one was being treated unfairly. It was hard on both of us, but it gave us a sense of justice. Karen was angry about the insinuation that her budget was excessive. Myles was angry about the prospect of disclosure. However, each realized the other was going to have to give a little. Karen would have to come down some on the budget, and Myles was finally going to have to tell her just how much they really had. The next session, the mediator further explained, would deal with reaching an agreement on child and spousal support based on all the facts, including needs, wants, adjusted budgets, and the actual financial disclosure of available property and money.

We both left the session in an angry and defensive state of mind. We were emotionally and physically tired. The session had been extremely stressful. We were both in a state of disbelief; it was hard to imagine that it would all be settled after our next session. It still seemed as if we were way too far apart. What possible basis for agreement did we have?

*Myles:* I was angry and fearful about the need to disclose the finances, and about the fact that Karen's needs and wants were so far above what I felt was reasonable or what I could effectively handle. I left this session fantasizing that somehow a miracle would happen or that I would be able to intimidate her to the point where she would cave in to my demands.

*Karen:* I was furious at Myles for using his "look how much I'm denying myself" routine to get sympathy from the mediator. I was scared about the financial position in which I would ultimately find myself. I resented being looked at as just another moneygrubbing wife and was afraid of having my budget so reduced that I would be unable to meet expenses. I also didn't know how much of our finances Myles would really divulge. How would I know he was telling the truth? How would I ever get across the point that the money wasn't his, but ours?

We were both very anxious, and very angry at each other. The tensions just kept on increasing during the two weeks. It was hard to talk to each other. The outlook was bleak, and we began to feel it really wasn't worth it. After all, we probably would end up in court anyway.

CHAPTER 10

# Organizing Financial Information

**F**inances play an important part in our lives whether we like it or not. In a divorce, the bottom line is usually money. Frequently one income, at least at the start, will have to support two households. Adjustments in life-styles, reduced budgets, and a reappraisal of available finances are necessary. Financial insecurity, which is discomforting for anyone, is intensified during a divorce.

To minimize the anxieties and make it possible to work out a settlement, both parties need to understand fully what their financial resources are. The more exact they can be about what they have to work with, the more effectively they can work out an agreement. They will be less overwhelmed and more able to deal with the future if they know the facts.

## What This Chapter Gives You

There are several reasons for this chapter. First, it provides worksheets to help you determine what you currently have, what you will have after the separation/divorce, and what you need for the future. Second, it demonstrates how highly organized mediation is. As you look over the forms and worksheets, you may get a feel for how useful this structure can be in making sense out of what seems to be an impossible task.

We have provided the forms, which we created as a result of our own working-through of our financial situation, so that you can familiarize yourself with how the process works. We want you to feel confident that both people are protected, and that all financial matters will be covered by the mediation session on financial conditions.

You are instrumental in this process. You are not going to sit back and let someone else do it for you. There is a set of tasks that must be done to reach the final settlement. You will find that if you work out each step, an agreement will be realized. It may take time to gather all the information, so it will be important to begin without delay once mediation has been agreed on. Also, as cooperation is fostered, more of the information will be gathered jointly. You are not in this alone.

The chapter will also show you how to go about getting much of the information you will need without outside help. The mediator will offer direction in locating needed facts and in filling out the forms.

There may be some people reading this book who are considering the possibility of a separation or divorce in the future. If that is the case, they can use this section (as well as other parts of the book) to find out valuable information that will prepare them for future eventualities. Knowing what assets and liabilities you have may cause you to reevaluate your plans or to at least be more realistic about how a divorce might affect your future. Our objective is to help you be more informed about your financial situation. This information is important for you no matter what you do.

The basis of this chapter is a set of worksheets to use to identify and organize your financial data. The chapter also includes worksheets to help you plot out your monthly budget. Completing these sheets will give you a starting point from which to begin to negotiate your financial settlement.

In addition, this chapter provides some suggestions on how to go about finding most of the information you will need. The mediator will guide you, but it will help if you prepare them yourself as much as possible.

We are not accountants, but we have tried to be as thorough as possible about the information you will need to have. We hope you will find the forms useful. Because the information required is basic to most divorces, there is a similarity between the forms we have provided and those used by other mediators. Feel free to use the forms or change them to suit your needs.

It is common for one spouse to be almost totally uninformed about the financial status of the marriage. While this may not be critical during a functioning marriage (although we feel it is not advisable), it can be devastating if a divorce occurs. It is true that mediation has, as one of its primary objectives, the development of each spouse as a separately functioning individual, both emotionally and financially; however, it can be a rude awakening for a woman (it most often is the woman) if she has allowed herself to be so uninformed that she must begin at the point of finding out how much her husband earns. This happens much more often than you would expect.

The following suggestions for obtaining financial information are not only meant for couples contemplating a divorce, but also to help make people aware that knowing the financial condition of their marriage is not frightening. It is part of being an equal partner in the relationship. It will reduce unrealistic expectations and fears. The more you know in advance, the less you will be traumatized if the status of your marriage changes—whether by separation, divorce, or by death of a spouse.

## Financial Data You Should Have

The most important document you can obtain is a copy of your *income tax return*. If you have filed jointly, you can write to the Internal Revenue Service for a "Request for a Copy of a Tax Return" form. If you keep a record of your past returns, you will probably have just about all the information you need regarding your financial situation. Information about salary, investment, interest on bank accounts, real estate owned, and other assets is available from these forms. Information on corporate taxes is also available since it is public record. You can get information about your spouse's corporate earnings if you need to. Many professionals form corporations, so if your spouse is a doctor or lawyer, for example, you might want to be aware of whether or not he is incorporated.

Another important area that you should be aware of is *pension and retirement funds* to which your spouse is contributing. These are considered marital property, even though only one spouse is contributing. Try to obtain an up-to-date picture of what the present value of the investment is. Get information on what will be paid at maturity. Be aware that if your spouse is not entitled to Social Security, by virtue of his profession, you may be left unprotected if retirement funds are not maintained. The situation on this score should be evaluated at the time of the separation/divorce.

Keep a record of all *joint savings and checking accounts*. Have the account numbers, bank addresses, and balances on file. Keep bank statements or copies of statements for your records. The tax returns will have a list of all accounts and interest that has accrued. Check for personal accounts that you may have been unaware of.

You should also have current knowledge of *credit card purchases and payments.* If the cards are in both names, you are entitled to copies of all bills. You can contact the credit card companies individually for copies of past statements. It is important for you to be aware of credit card debts for which you may be held partly responsible if a separation/divorce occurs. Also, if items were purchased on credit for a spouse's office or personal use, these items may need to be included as part of the marital property at some future time.

If you know that you and your spouse own *stocks, bonds, funds, or other securities,* try to have a record of the purchases and sales. It is important that you know the firm or broker that your spouse generally deals with. The tax returns will show the items purchased and sold, but being able to contact the broker will provide quick, personal information on any activity that has been taking place related to your holdings. These items are marital property unless purchased before marriage, even if your name is not on them. If you have a record of the stocks or commodities that have been purchased since your marriage, you can check the newspaper and get an idea of the value and the activity of the stock. If these are steps you have not been taking, it still may not be too late. You can begin now to take an active role in the financial activities of your family, so you will have the data you need whenever you need it.

Another form you will want to have is the *state tax returns.* You can write for this as well. You may find items such as tax-exempt bonds that are listed on the state form but not on the federal form.

Keep a record of all *insurance policies.* List the company, name, identification number, type of policy, and amount. It is also helpful to have a record of the renewal dates and amounts of the premiums. Include life, health, disability, car, home, fire, and any other policy you own. Have a record of who the beneficiaries are and if there are any outstanding loans against any of the policies. If you have this information ahead of time, countless hours of hunting and waiting will be saved when you find you need it. You don't have to be in the dark until your spouse turns over all the relevant data.

Another point to consider is that you are also responsible for *debts and loans accumulated during the marriage.* If you have co-signed any loans, whether they are for your spouse's business or for home improvement loans, you may have forgotten about them if your spouse writes the payment checks. Nevertheless, they are half yours. Try to maintain a record of all loans that either of you has made during the marriage. Even if you haven't signed them, they are part of marital property.

Much of this information may be "after the fact." If you have kept records throughout your marriage, you are a major step ahead of most couples. If not, you can begin now. You may need to start from scratch to gather the information you need, but this is not impossible to do.

Mediation relies on the willingness of both spouses to participate, sharing information openly. We therefore assume that the information you need will be given cooperatively by your spouse, or that you will work together to collect it. We feel that even if for some reason you choose not to use mediation, this section (and others), will still serve as an excellent source of self-help. We also recommend that you read some of the books and articles listed in the bibliography. These will provide more detailed information on finances and budgeting.

Date _____    Name _____

# I. CALCULATION OF INCOME

|                                          | Husband        | Wife           |
|------------------------------------------|----------------|----------------|
| **Gross Salary:** from primary source    | _____  | _____  |
| Less deductions                          | _____  | _____  |
|   a.  Federal tax              | _____  | _____  |
|   b.  State tax                | _____  | _____  |
|   c.  City tax                 | _____  | _____  |
|   d.  FICA or Retirement       | _____  | _____  |
|   Insurance, payroll, savings, etc. | _____ | _____ |
|   Other                        | _____  | _____  |
| NET INCOME FROM SALARY                   | $_____  | $_____  |

Additions

  a.  Dividends from:
    Bank savings accounts
    Stocks and bonds
    Money market funds
    CD's, all savers certificates
    Other

  b.  Rental income

  c.  Accounts receivable—loans
    due you (if regularly paid)

  d.  Income from other business
    interests

  e.  Copyrights, royalties, trade-
    marks

  f.  Income from trusts

  g.  Support payments to you from
    other marriage(s)

  h.  Tax refunds

  i.  Pension/annuity/disability

  j.  Social Security

  k.  Other sources not included

*Subtractions*

a. Estimated taxes due _____ _____

b. Self-employment taxes _____ _____

c. Other deductions for tax payments or income not subject to
withholding _____ _____

d. Dependent deductions _____ _____

e. Other—specify _____ _____

TOTAL DEDUCTIONS $_____ $_____

**Actual Yearly Take Home**

+Total Annual Income $_____ $_____

−less Total Deductions $_____ $_____

Actual Annual Income $_____ $_____

Actual Monthly Income $_____ $_____

# II. ASSETS

## Cash in Bank Accounts
*(prepare table for each account)*

☐ Savings   ☐ Checking   ☐ Other

Type _____

Name on account _____

Account No. _____

Balance _____

Location _____

## Children's Bank Accounts
*(prepare table for each account)*

Type _____

Name on account _____

Account No. _____

Balance _____

Location _____

## Other Interest-Bearing Accounts, Funds, etc.

☐ *Joint*   ☐ *Individual* _____
*(prepare table for each account or fund)*

Type _____

Name on account _____

Account No. _____

Balance _____

Location _____

## Money Owed to You

☐ *Joint* ☐ *Individual* _____
*(prepare table for each debt)*

☐ Loans ☐ Accounts Receivable ☐ Rental ☐ Other

Form _____

Debtor _____

Balance Due _____

Payment Schedule _____

## Other Business Income

☐ *Joint* ☐ *Individual* _____
*(prepare a table for each)*

Business name and location _____

Percent of ownership _____

Date of first involvement _____

Actual money invested _____

Loans initiated by you _____

Your value in it _____

Stock options _____

Projected investment needs _____

Estimated monthly income _____
*(Will need buy-sell agreement, profit and loss statement and tax returns for each business.)*

## Patent, Trademark, Copyright Interests

☐ *Joint* ☐ *Individual* _____
*(prepare table for each)*

Type _____

Effective date _____

Income generated _____

Your investment _____

Loans against _____

Estimated worth _____

## Pensions and Other Retirement Accounts
*(prepare table for each account)*

Name of plan _____

Name on plan _____

Effective date _____

Percent vested _____

Distribution _____

Present value _____

Projected value at retirement _____

## Real Estate Owned
*(prepare table for each piece of real estate)*

Location _____

Name on deed _____

Date _____

Type _____

Original cost _____

Current value _____

Mortgage amount _____

Date due _____

## Real Estate Mortgages Owned

☐ *Joint*   ☐ *Individual* _____
*(prepare table for each)*

Location _____

Type _____

Type of lien _____

Mortgagee _____

Original amount _____

Present amount _____

Date of maturity _____

Type of payment _____

TOTAL OF ASSETS  $ _____

# III. LIST OF PERSONAL EFFECTS
*(prepare table for every item)*

Type:   ☐ Boat   ☐ Plane   ☐ Automobiles   ☐ Recreational Vehicle
☐ Art   ☐ Jewelry   ☐ Other

Describe item _____

Present value _____

Estimated rate of growth in value _____

In whose name _____

Who uses it most _____

How acquired _____

Where located _____

Insurance coverage _____

Money invested _____

Money still owed _____

Purpose _____

etc. _____


# IV. HOUSEHOLD FURNISHINGS

☐ Joint   ☐ Individual _____
*(prepare table for each room in dwelling)*

Item _____

Date purchased _____

Original cost _____

Present value _____

Form of payment _____

Who uses it most _____

How acquired _____

# V. LIFE INSURANCE POLICIES
*(prepare table for every policy)*

Policy type _____

Policy number_____

Company_____

Face amount_____

Beneficiary _____

Death benefit_____

Type of policy_____

Loans against_____

Cash value_____

Premiums_____


# VI. OTHER INSURANCE POLICIES
*(prepare table for every policy)*

Type:   ☐ Homeowners   ☐ Renters   ☐ Health   ☐ Auto

☐ Accident   ☐ Others _____

Type of Insurance_____

Company_____

Policy number_____

Name of insured_____

Expiration date _____

Premium_____

Benefits _____

Other pertinent information _____

# VII. LIST OF MISCELLANEOUS ASSETS

Gifts anticipated for child/children _____

Gifts anticipated for either spouse _____

Inheritance expected for child/children _____

Safety deposit box contents _____

Cemetary plot(s) _____

Expected future Social Security _____

TOTAL ASSETS $ _____

# VIII. ESTIMATE OF LIABILITIES

Notes payable to banks _____

Notes payable to relatives _____

Notes payable to friends/others _____

Accounts payable _____

Installment loans _____

Federal and state income taxes payable _____

Other taxes and interest _____

Mortgages payable _____

Loans against life insurance _____

Credit card accounts—*list separately on separate page, identifying account names and number along with amount owed and current payment procedure.* _____

TOTAL LIABILITIES PER MONTH _____

TOTAL GROSS LIABILITIES _____

# IX. CALCULATION OF NET WORTH

*Total Assets* $_____

*Total Liabilities* $_____

NET WORTH $_____

# X. CALCULATION OF LIABILITIES

## Notes Payable to Banks

☐ *Joint*   ☐ *Individual* _____
*(Separate sheet for each loan)*

Name of bank _____

Date and original loan amount _____

Balance remaining _____

Monthly payment _____

Purpose of loan _____

Name of any cosigner _____

Method of borrowing _____
*(Unsecured, secured, guaranteed, etc.)*

## Mortgages or Real Estate
*(Separate sheet for each item)*

Location of property _____

Type _____

When purchased _____

Names appearing on title _____

Original cost _____

Source of original purchase funds _____

Current appraised value _____

Mortgage amount _____

Monthly payments _____

Date due _____

Balance remaining/Number of payments remaining _____
*Specify if there are any other liens against the above listed property, and if any payments or taxes are in arrears. Explain.*

## Notes Payable to Friends or Relatives/Others

☐ *Joint*   ☐ *Individual* _____
*(prepare table for each)*

Creditor _____

Purpose _____

Date of loan _____

Present balance _____

Monthly payments _____

Type of loan _____

Cosigner if any _____

## Contingent Debts, Accounts Payable, Installment Loans, Contracts Payable

☐ *Joint*   ☐ *Individual* _____
*(prepare table for each)*

Creditor _____

Purpose _____

Balance due _____

Monthly payment _____

Describe contingencies _____

## TAXES

☐ *Federal*   ☐ *State*   ☐ *Local*

☐ *Joint*   ☐ *Individual* _____
*(prepare table for each)*

Taxing party _____

Date incurred _____

Balance due _____

Monthly or periodic payments *(specify period)* _____

## Loans Against Life Insurance Policies

□ *Joint*   □ *Individual* _____
*(prepare table for each policy)*

Policy number _____

Type of policy _____

Face value _____

Beneficiary _____

Amount of loan _____

Balance remaining _____

## Other Liabilities

□ *Joint*   □ *Individual* _____
*(prepare table for each)*

Creditor _____

Purpose _____

Date _____

Original amount _____

Remaining balance _____

Monthly payments _____

Secured/unsecured _____

Comments/explanation _____

Payments to children of earlier marriage(s) _____

Payments to spouse(s) from earlier marriage(s) _____

TOTAL LIABILITIES $ _____

# XI. EXPENSE BUDGET ESTIMATES

## Regular Monthly Expenses
### Home

| | Single | Child(ren) |
|---|---|---|
| Mortgage payments | | |
|     Principal | | |
|     Interest | | |
|     Taxes | | |
|     Insurance | | |
| Rental payments | | |
| Condominium fee | | |
| Home Insurance | | |
| Other *(specify)* | | |

### Utilities

| | Single | Child(ren) |
|---|---|---|
| Electricity | | |
| Gas/Heating oil | | |
| Telephone | | |
| Water and sewer | | |
| Hot water *(if separate)* | | |
| Septic tank service | | |
| Other *(specify)* | | |

### House maintenance

| | Single | Child(ren) |
|---|---|---|
| *Outside* | | |
| Lawn and yard upkeep | | |
| Landscaping | | |
| External repairs | | |
| Garbage service | | |
| Snow removal | | |
| Other | | |

*Inside*

Domestic assistance _____ _____

Cleaning supplies _____ _____

Special cleaning carpets/windows _____ _____

Repair/replacement _____ $ _____

Furniture repair _____ _____

Other _____ _____


**Insurance**

Life _____ _____

Disability _____ _____

Health _____ _____

Accident _____ _____

Other _____ _____


**Installment debts** _____ _____
(List separately)

Creditor _____ _____

Purpose _____ _____

Payments _____ _____

Balance _____ _____


**Membership dues**

Union _____ _____

Professional organizations _____ _____

Clubs _____ _____

Religious institutions/groups _____ _____

Other _____ _____

TOTAL MONTHLY EXPENSES   $ _____   $ _____

# Daily Expenses

### Food

Home _____    _____

School _____    _____

Work _____    _____

Meals out _____    _____

### Clothing and shoes

Yourself _____    _____

Children _____    _____

Alterations _____    _____

Cleaning _____    _____

### Transportation

Car payments _____    _____

Gas/oil _____    _____

Tune-ups _____    _____

Tires _____    _____

Repairs/oil change _____    _____

Parking fees _____    _____

Vehicle parking stickers _____    _____

Commuter stickers _____    _____

Property tax stickers _____    _____

County/local/State tags _____    _____

Periodic inspections _____    _____

Bus/taxi/train _____    _____

Plane _____    _____

Car insurance _____    _____

Other _____    _____

**Medical**

Insurance premiums  _____  _____

Bills not covered by insurance  _____  _____

Dental/Orthodontics  _____  _____

Counseling  _____  _____

Eyeglasses/hearing aids/etc.  _____  _____

Prescriptions  _____  _____

Medical supplies  _____  _____

Other  _____  _____

**Education**

School tuition  _____  _____

Religious school  _____  _____

College  _____  _____

Graduate programs  _____  _____

Vocational training  _____  _____

Special training  _____  _____

Living expenses  _____  _____

Books  _____  _____

School supplies  _____  _____

Special fees  _____  _____

Extracurricular activities  _____  _____

**Allowances**

Yourself  _____  _____

Child (ren)  _____  _____

TOTAL DAILY EXPENSES  $_____  $_____

## Other Expenses

**Recreational**

Newspapers/magazines/newsletters _____ _____

Records _____ _____

Books _____ _____

Pictures _____ _____

Art _____ _____

Hobby supplies _____ _____

Photo supplies _____ _____

Bicycle _____ _____

Bicycle supplies _____ _____

Lessons *(list)* _____ _____

Clubs/teams *(list)* _____ _____

Swimming pool/club memberships _____ _____

Pets/pet supplies _____ _____

Boy/Girl Scouts _____ _____

Parties _____ _____

Special occasions/celebrations _____ _____

Family outings _____ _____

Movies _____ _____

Dates _____ _____

Theater/concerts _____ _____

Gifts *(specify)* _____ _____

**Personal Expenses**

Hair _____ _____

Sitters/day care _____ _____

Summer camp _____ _____

Other *(list)* _____ _____

**Charitable contributions**

Religious                                    _____      _____

Medical                                      _____      _____

School                                       _____      _____

College                                      _____      _____

Other *(specify)*                            _____      _____


**Incidentals**

*(Itemize)*                                  _____      _____


**Other/Miscellaneous** *(specify)*          _____      _____

TOTAL VARIABLE EXPENSES      $_____    $_____


# Money for Emergencies, Unforeseen Events, Planned Future Events
*(prepare tables for each as necessary)*
- ☐ *Emergency*
- ☐ *Savings Acct.*
- ☐ *Retirement*
- ☐ *Automobile saving*
- ☐ *Major appl.*
- ☐ *Vacation*
- ☐ *Special investment*
- ☐ *Holiday savings*
- ☐ *Special occasions not otherwise included*
- ☐ *Other (specify)*

Purpose_____

Estimated cost _____

Dated needed _____

Per month _____

Per year_____

TOTAL ADDITIONAL EXPENSES  $_____

## ESTIMATED EXPENSES—TOTALS

Total Regular Monthly Expenses $_____

Total Daily Living Expenses $_____

Total Variable Expenses$_____

Total Additional Expenses $_____

TOTAL ESTIMATED MONTHLY NEEDS _____

CHAPTER 11

# Financial Support
## Our Mediation

The tension had been building up over the weeks before the meeting. We both realized that this session would determine whether or not the process was going to be successful. Because of how we both felt at the time, neither one of us really believed it would work. We each had preconceived ideas of what would happen. We hassled over Karen's basic financial needs, but no matter what Myles suggested decreasing, Karen seemed unwilling to change her position. This only angered and frustrated Myles further. He had already established in his mind the limit on how much he would give, and there was no way Karen was going to be able to change that limit.

Nevertheless, we both had already reached the conclusion that one way or another, virtually everything would be settled at this session. If neither gave in, both had the ultimate weapon in reserve—walking out and going to court.

Despite all the anxieties, we both found that for the first time, we were learning how to negotiate for ourselves. A result of this was that we each came into this session with a plan of how we were going to achieve our objectives. Myles had talked to some attorneys and was advised that what Karen wanted per month was out of line, and that the amount he was willing to give was probably too high as well. Based on this advice, he decided that he would definitely maintain his limit to how much he would pay per month.

*Myles:* During the two intervening weeks, we did discuss splitting the property. Though Karen was basically uninformed about what our resources were, I got a good idea of what I thought she would accept. I planned on offering her a little more of the property in exchange for lower monthly payments. Of course, I never told her that.

Whenever we argued during this period, I would always threaten to forget the whole thing. After all, I felt I could ultimately get a better deal in court—but I wanted to be "fair." If Karen pushed me too far, then off to court I was willing to go. When she acted as if this would be just fine with her and said that she would stick to her position, I retorted that if worse came to worse and I was forced to pay her that much, I just wouldn't work. Then there would be nothing to negotiate at all.

*Karen:* I knew Myles had a strong sense of insecurity about finances, but I wasn't ready to let that influence my objectives. The major problem was that I really didn't know what the total resources were. I wasn't aware of all the marital property except for the funds we had been contributing to for some time. Myles wanted all of the funds, and I felt I was entitled to half as part of what had been our shared resources for the future. I also wanted the townhouse in which I was living, part of the savings, and my car. I knew Myles well enough not to let him know how scared I was when he threatened me. I knew that in front of the mediator he couldn't dominate me, so I fought back and stood up to him for the first time in my life. I also acted as if it was fine with me if we went to court. I actually had both an attorney and friends tell me that I was not getting what I really deserved and that I could do much better in court. So I, too, had established a bottom line.

## Positive Feelings
Surprisingly, both of us were beginning to get a positive feeling within ourselves despite all the outward anxiety and frustration. Karen realized she was able to stand up to Myles and not be intimidated by him. Myles started to feel confident that he would be able to negotiate a settlement. He felt good knowing that there was a way to gain control of his life and, no matter what anyone said, he felt he was being fair. He felt proud of this.

We wanted this to work. We had already invested a lot of time and effort in mediation. We had agreed to certain key issues, and we were both growing independently. Deep down, we both preferred not to have to resort to the courts. Our accomplishments would seem wasted if we gave up at this point. Finally, we began to understand that, like it or not, because of the children we would have to continue our relationship as parents even after the divorce—probably for the rest of our lives. Life was hard enough without the bitterness that was likely to result from giving up now.

## Going Over Karen's Budget

When we arrived at the session, the mediator had prepared a large chart on the easel. All items Karen listed on her monthly expense sheet were exhibited, with blank columns next to them. The mediator suggested that all three of us go over each item and concentrate on its meaning with a view toward being realistic.

Myles at first was reluctant. Karen was tense. We did it anyway. When we were all through, the figures still came out higher than Myles was willing to pay. Karen indicated that she could not make ends meet on what he offered. At this point, Myles presented his bottom line and refused to discuss it further. Karen seemed ready to give in until the mediator pointed out that she would be taxed on a large portion of the payments; consequently, the available money would be less than the figures shown on the paper. Since most of the money would be paid as alimony, Myles would get a tax break at her expense. Karen then refused to back off and refused to go lower than a figure that was higher than Myles' final rebuttal offer.

Myles then erupted again. He pleaded with her and with the mediator. He said that he fully intended to take care of Karen and the children, but he too needed some financial security. He honestly felt he wouldn't be able to handle giving her more than he had suggested. Since he felt this way, if they both disagreed, he didn't see any sense in continuing. He would have to take his chances in court. As far as he was concerned, he might as well stop working and living, because there would be nothing left for him. He also brought up the fact that he had been offered a position in another state for less income than he was presently making. Even though he wouldn't see his children as much, he would consider the new position. Karen would then have to take less. Karen was aware of this offer; however, she knew him well enough to be confident that this ploy was just hot air. It was a last-ditch attempt to win over the mediator's sympathy. She refused to back down.

## The Mediator Intervenes

The mediator then went into a detailed discussion of the tax laws. If Myles would take advantage of them he could give Karen more.

Ultimately he would still benefit, because the payments could serve as a large tax write-off. He could both respond to Karen's needs and still come out ahead. Myles refused to be moved. He was so angry that he didn't listen and didn't understand what the mediator was saying. The mediator himself became frustrated. Karen was sitting quietly, pretending to be calm, taking her notes. This only made Myles more agitated.

The mediator explained to Myles that the purpose of mediation was to settle the legal issues of divorce, and also to prepare both people for an independent life. The payments were to include tuition for Karen to go back to graduate school to receive training in connection with her career goals, so she could map out an independent professional life for herself, as she had assisted Myles in doing for his professional life. With this approach, the payments would eventually be reduced to just child support once Karen had accomplished her educational goals. Now it was Karen's turn to get upset.

The mediator explained it all a second time. Myles refused to listen or to go any further. He stood up and started to walk out. We were given a few minutes to cool off.

## Financial Disclosure

The mediator suggested that we leave this issue at the present figure for the time being, and go on to financial disclosure and division of property. Maybe progress could be made in that area.

Myles recalls considering concealing some information about what resources we had accumulated, since things looked pretty bleak anyway. Why tell her what she really didn't know, especially if they could end up in court. He was angry at himself for having put both names on everything. When friends had jokingly said years before, "...if she doesn't suggest it, forget it." He had said, "don't worry, we'll never get divorced."

The mediator asked us to list all the property that we had acquired together, including all our investments, bank accounts, stocks, and other resources.

## Division of Property

After all was written down, the mediator told us that the usual approach was to divide the resources equally. In our case, there were two additional reasons for taking this course: first, it was obvious that

Karen had helped Myles develop his career and deserved half of what they had; second, it would minimize the tax consequences if they each were to receive equal amounts of their acquired worth.

There were very emotional exchanges as we negotiated for the division of all property and resources. Karen was upset because she felt the stocks and bonds would be worth a lot more in the future even though they were currently equal in value to the house and the cash in the bank. Myles responded that she had requested that he cover the children's future college expenses. He was willing to do so, and therefore needed the chance to build up the necessary resources to meet those future costs.

Myles wanted some of the cash in the bank and also knew that Karen had a small sum in her own personal account that she had saved over the years. He wanted this included as part of their overall bank account assets. He also wanted some of the furniture, but it didn't have enough value to even be considered. All the furniture was old and of little financial value, but Karen felt her resources were limited. She couldn't afford to purchase anything new.

As the discussions wore on, it became obvious to all that most of the controversy was a way of expressing the tension and hostility we had both built up concerning the support issues discussed at the beginning of the session. We still finally hammered out an agreement.

Karen would get the townhouse, furniture, her car, the entire savings account, and life and health insurance coverage for each child.

Myles would get all their stocks and bonds and his car, and Karen would have no involvement in his professional practice or in other business ventures that he had gotten involved in while they were separated.

Even though we showed little outward enthusiasm about the property distribution, we were both actually comfortable with it. However, we both knew that the worst was still to come. Neither of us wanted to appear too positive in case that would allow the other to get the upper hand. The exchange had been very hard on us emotionally; we were both drained.

## A Second Try at Financial Support Issues

The mediator congratulated us both and suggested that since there was time left, we ought to try and discuss the financial support issues again.

He reiterated the potential tax implications to Myles if he were allowed to give most of the payment in the form of alimony; however, Karen would have to be taxed, so Myles should be willing to give her a little more. On the other hand, Karen should realize some of her figures were too high, that Myles didn't have unlimited funds, and that her life-style might have to be adjusted somewhat, Myles had furnished the previous three years federal and state tax returns to document salaries and investments. All the facts were now out in the open.

The mediator pointed out that the issue of support payments was all that remained to complete the agreement. It would be a shame not to try and cooperate, listen to the other side, and finally work it out. He also pointed to all of the positive accomplishments we had achieved so far. We had obviously come a long way, and we knew that if we didn't finish it here, the lawyers and the courts would have to do it for us further down the road.

The mediator was certainly aware of our nervousness, our exhaustion, and our exasperation. Actually, we both wanted to leave, to put off any further discussion until next session. The mediator, however, because of his experience, knew that this was the time to continue. We were tense and uptight. We knew either consciously or unconsciously that if we could reach an agreement we could just about complete the process. Perhaps the inability of either of us to face the divorce was playing a larger part in blocking our efforts than we thought. After a little while, we both consented to continue.

**Our Communications Improve**—After some honest communication about our real reasons for being inflexible about the proposed financial settlement, we both found out that we were very frightened of having to trust one another. In fact, we were both really afraid of the same thing—financial insecurity. We each understood how the other felt and we said so to one another. We also thanked one another for the property settlement that each had received.

Karen was still petrified at the thought of having to be financially independent for the first time in her life. She felt that if the payments were dropped after two to three years, she wouldn't be able to make it. She also wanted a cost-of-living increase.

Myles did listen to her. He knew she wasn't trying to get away with everything. She was really frightened about having to become responsible for her own financial needs. She was not trying to deceive him.

Karen's statement about the cost-of-living increase struck a sensitive nerve in Myles. This time, however, instead of exploding, he calmly told her how sorry he was and that he believed her; but as insecure as she would feel without a cost-of-living factor, he would be equally insecure with one. He also tried to show her how he didn't want to leave her destitute, that as long as he did well he would see to it that she and the children were well-supported.

The mediator suggested that we both consider five years as a reasonable period for Karen to get her training completed. She had decided to get a Master's degree in Human Resources and had figured out how much it would cost per year. The mediator took her figures, which had already been reviewed, added in her graduate school tuition costs plus an approximate figure for taxes each quarter, and came up with a figure that Myles thought was reasonable, but that Karen thought was too low.

Myles was of the opinion that five years at the original amount per month was too long, especially because Karen would graduate in two years and would be able to generate income herself. Karen was then willing to consider diminished payments after three years with only child support to continue after five years. She felt reasonably secure with this arrangement. This would give her time to build towards self-suifficiency.

**Agreements are Reached**—After additional discussion, we finally agreed on the five-year plan—high payments initially, decreasing after the third and fourth year. In exchange for this arrangement, Karen would not get a cost-of-living increase because of Myles's inability to cope with it. In addition, Karen was to be responsible for all other financial support of the children, such as camps, clubs, clothes, and participation in any other extracurricular activities like soccer, tennis, and religious school. No additional money would come from Myles to cover these expenses.

To ease Karen's anxieties, Myles offered to buy a larger life insurance policy for her than she had requested and had the following items written into the agreement:

(1) He would provide sole support of the children after they reached eighteen years of age, no matter who had what money or was married to whom.

(2) He would never use this financial control over the children to manipulate them away from her.

(3) If Karen was in dire financial condition, she could come to him first—if he had money he would loan it to her: if he required a payback, it would be without interest.

(4) He would cover her gas and car maintenance payments.

Although Karen was to pay for camp and other outside activities, Myles could have a say in decisions concerning those activities. Also, they would both participate in the decision about what colleges the children would eventually attend, assuming they decided to go.

## What Was Next

Somehow we had gotten through it. We had been working for at least two hours. We both remember getting up feeling wobbly-legged, weak, and exhausted. It had been a terribly draining experience. The mediator then told us that the next step was to meet with an independent tax consultant who was familiar with mediation, divorce law, and tax implications. He gave us the names of several; we both were to agree on one, and to see him independently. He would then send a written report to Karen, Myles, and the mediator. The tax consultant would receive from the mediator a copy of the basic agreement. This would be called the *Memorandum of Agreement.* The accountant's report would be called the *Tax Consultation Memorandum.*

The date for the next session was set for several weeks in the future to give us time to get the report from the mediator, consult with the financial advisor, and meet with the independent accountants and/or lawyers. By the time we returned for the next session, the mediator would have taken the above two memoranda and combined them into an initial draft of our final memorandum of agreement.

With a sigh of relief and a good deal of sadness, we left. This had been the most difficult session, but it had provided proof of the positive results of mediation. Reaching financial decisions that we both were comfortable with, gave us confidence that we could work through the many difficult issues to come. We both felt that, since these were not externally imposed decisions, we would be able to live up to our commitments.

CHAPTER 12

# Completing The Divorce Procedure

Once all the issues have been dealt with and all negotiating has been completed, the preliminary agreement is written out by the mediator in the form of a *memorandum of agreement*. The mediator reviews all the issues with the couple present. When all parties are satisfied with the contents, it is ready to be written out in a formal legal document that will serve as a legal separation agreement and ultimately may be part of the final divorce agreement, the divorce decree.

As with all other stages of mediation, there are specific guidelines to get this accomplished. The mediator gives the couple a choice of several advisory attorneys. These are lawyers who have not been involved in the process up to this point. They are familiar with mediation, divorce law, and the tax consequences of divorce law. Their job is to give legal advice and translate your agreement into a legal document.

## Mediator's Approval

Before this final review is made, the mediator will usually look over the agreement with the idea of giving it her approval. Usually the mediator approves the agreement; however, there are times when she will not agree, on the grounds that is not fair to one or both of the parties involved. She may also object because she thinks that it is just not workable. Such a lack of approval does not invalidate the agreement, but it could have an impact if for some reason it is ever challenged in court.

This final review also serves as a way that the mediator and the mediation center she represents can protect themselves or their reputations. One example might be a case where the husband has a limited income, but is so guilt-ridden that he agrees to pay a larger amount of support than he can reasonably afford.

## What is Done When Participants have Doubts about the Settlement?

If one of the participants who has worked through the settlement has doubts about it, then he can request that a special evaluation session be held. In this session, the mediator and the advisory attorney give their opinions as to whether it is an appropriate agreement or not. They go over what they see as the advantages and disadvantages, and they compare it to other agreements they have been involved with that involve similar circumstances. The participants can call for this review at any time. Technically, they may do so again after the final form of the document is prepared by the advisory attorney.

Another option is to seek independent legal, tax, or acccounting advice at any stage one desires. The mediator reminds the couple that this may be done at various points along the way.

## Revisions

If revisions are to be made, they can be made in one of two ways. If they are minor, they can be done right then and there. Or, if the mediator feels that these changes should not be decided under pressure of time, she may call for an additional session to renegotiate the issues in question.

The advisory attorney is someone familiar with the process and not biased toward either party in any way. He is neutral as the mediator is. He may not be hired or consulted by either spouse for their individual interests for a period of one year after the agreement is signed. However, he may, if mutually agreed on, represent one of them for the purpose of procuring a settlement agreement, or for filing for divorce using the agreement reached through mediation.

In some situations, one lawyer is called in to do the work of the advisory attorney as described above. In other situations a tax consultant (either an accountant or an attorney) is used to handle the tax ramifications of the agreement, and is then followed by a second consultant who serves as the advisory attorney.

There may be situations where other specialized consultants are needed. These additional consultants will of course have to be mutually agreed on by the mediation participants, and may or may not have to be recommended by the mediator. Examples would be a jewelry or art appriaser or a real-estate appraiser. All their findings are documented and become part of the mediation file. Copies are sent to both parties and to the mediator. If indicated, their recommendations will be incorporated into the written memorandum of agreement prepared by the mediator.

## Understanding the Tax Implications of Your Agreement

The next step is to go over the financial aspects of the agreement with the advisory attorney or a tax consultant. In either case, the purpose is for each of you to understand the tax implications of what you have agreed to, and to take advantage of existing federal and state tax laws. For example, under the Lester Rule, most of the support money can be paid by the husband to the wife in the form of alimony. This could represent a significant tax advantage to the husband. The wife would, however, be taxed on the alimony as income. Cooperation between spouses in this case can lead to benefits for both—tax advantages for the one paying support, and increased payments for the one receiving the support.

Another situation is when the property is split fifty/fifty. This minimizes tax consequences to one party or another, since no taxable event will have occurred. Finally, it is often advisable to bequest a house or a car as a gift to one spouse or the other, depending again on the overall financial situation. The key point is that there is a lot that can be done to soften the financial blow to both sides. Proper advice is important.

It is important to realize that in most cases there has to be an adjustment in life-styles to reflect the division of financial responsibility. What originally supported one household must now, at least temporarily, support two. The dependent spouse often assumes she can continue to live the same kind of life that existed before the separation and divorce. The independent spouse, on the other hand, often assumes he is now free to do all the things that couldn't be done before. In most cases, however, this just isn't what happens. The standard of living of both parties must change. You must expect this and adapt to it.

Each one of the participants meets with the advisory attorney or tax consultant to go over all the ramifications of the proposed agreement. All three people can meet together to do this. The consultant will explain her recommendations to the couple, guided by the finances at hand, the tax laws, and the needs of the participants. This process is for explanatory and review purposes, it is not meant as a renegotiation of agreements already reached. If you choose to use a tax consultant, she will then put what has been discussed in the form of a written report sent to each of the participants, the mediator, and the advisory attorney.

At this point in the process, you have the right to get independent advice from an accountant, attorney, or other consultant before going on. Either participant can ask for an evaluation session. This is to assure yourself that the negotiated settlement and recommendations so far reflect what you believe they should, and that the negotiation so far has been to the best advantage of both of you. This review also helps you avoid future misunderstandings. If you have used an advisory atorney for this review, he also will prepare and distribute a written report.

## The Draft of the Separation Agreement

What happens next is that the advisory attorney takes the memorandum of agreement that has been worked out with the mediator, along with the tax recommendations that have been worked out, and prepares a preliminary draft of the separation agreement.

After a few weeks time, you will both get copies of the preliminary separation agreement, and one copy will go to the mediator. You are advised to read this document carefully, and to seek independent counsel if desired. Note any corrections or changes; if necessary, you will both return to see the advisory attorney to discuss any proposed changes. If any major issues arise, you will be asked to return to the mediator. All changes must be agreed to by all parties.

## The Separation Agreement

Finally, once all is finished, you will each spend a few minutes alone with the advisory attorney at a set time and place. He will read over the entire final *Custody, Property and Separation Agreement* and answer any questions. Then you will both sign it in the presence of a notary public. At that point, the agreement becomes a legal document.

After you have been separated for the period of time required by your state laws, either of you can file for divorce. One of you can use the advisory attorney to file if mutually agreed on. If not, you can choose another attorney recommended by the mediator, or one outside of the process.

Since the legal separation document has settled all the issues, both parties do not have to appear in court. The spouse who filed must appear with legal representation and a witness. The other spouse may or may not appear. Also present are the magistrate of the court and a court stenographer. The magistrate reads through the agreement, verifies a few points, then on an assigned date, usually within a few weeks from the hearing, presents the information to the judge, who officially grants the divorce decree.

CHAPTER 13

# Preparation and Review of Draft Agreement

## Our Mediation

**S**hortly after the momentous session in which we actually completed negotiating the final aspects of our separation agreement, we each received a copy of a document called the Memorandum of Agreement. A copy was also sent to the financial consultant we had jointly chosen. Both of us were to look over this agreement separately to make sure that it contained what we had agreed to. If there was anything in this document that either of us didn't understand, agree with, or if there was anything we still wanted changed, we were to make a note about it so we could discuss it before or during our upcoming final session. In addition, the mediator suggested that either one of us who was so inclined consult with an independent attorney. Finally, we were to meet independently and jointly if necessary with the tax consultant we had contacted earlier.

### Myles's Meeting with the Tax Advisor
Myles went to see the tax advisor first. He was requested to furnish specific financial information. This information included financial disclosure documentation, back tax returns, and other relevant documentation. The advisor reviewed the agreement in detail, working out our financial support figures to maximize Myles's cash flow and minimize Karen's taxes. He also explained that it was important for both Myles and Karen to work out equal distribution of property if neither was to be faced with a sizable tax bill because of the impending divorce.

The tax consultant had a good deal of experience in these matters and was able to make concrete suggestions on exactly how to deal with the support and maintenance payments, life and health insurance payments, future college education expenses, future needs, and other property matters. He explained what he thought was reasonable and fair to both Myles and Karen and what his conclusions were based on.

During this meeting, Myles was most concerned about the exact amount he would have to give per month to cover the monthly support plus Karen's yearly tax liability. The accountant could only give an estimate of the tax figure, and it seemed it could go higher than had been anticipated during the mediation session. Myles insisted there be a ceiling on what he would pay toward her taxes. The accountant said he would work with the figures to see what the possibilities were.

As had been argued in the mediation sessions, Myles did not want any cost-of-living provision included in the agreement or any pyramiding of tax payments as a potential basis for increasing monthly payments. He also wanted some clarification as to what would happen if Karen decided to work and began to make a significant income. Finally, he wanted Karen to be completely responsible for all additional expenses relating to the children except for college. These expenses would include vacations other than those during which Myles had responsibility for the children, camps, athletic teams, and extra medical costs other than what the high-option insurance plans would cover.

This meeting ended with the tax consultant taking under advisement Myles's concerns and recommendations. He said he would prepare an unofficial memorandum based on this information and would work out an estimated income tax return for Karen for the upcoming year, the first year in which she would be filing separately. This would all be completed prior to his meeting with Karen, so that they could go over specific data, which would then be reviewed with Myles at a subsequent meeting.

## Karen's Meeting with the Tax Advisor

Karen met with the tax consultant a short time later, and additional problems began to emerge. She was not in agreement with the the idea of a tax ceiling, nor with the lack of a built-in cost-of-living increase. Finally, she insisted that Myles obtain a $100,000 life insurance policy as protection for the support payments that had been established.

Karen was also very concerned about the rate at which the payments were to decrease during the first five years. She wanted it to be as gradual as possible, to help prevent unforeseen financial problems, leaving her unable to complete her degree. Finally, she wanted a statement declaring her free of liability from any debts Myles might still have or might acquire prior to their official divorce.

## New Problems and Further Solutions

Things only seemed to be getting worse. We were scheduled for our last session, and that session was for the purpose of reviewing the first draft of the separation memorandum. This memorandum was to be drafted by the mediator, using his notes from our sessions and incorporating the advice of the tax consultant. We contacted the mediator independently, and he suggested postponing the last session awhile longer to give us another opportunity to work out our differences.

Judging from our track record, we were both pessimistic about our likelihood of being able to do so. However, we agreed to try. This time, we would attempt to reach a solution without the help of the mediator. No one would be there to protect Karen or to help prevent Myles from losing control emotionally. We were being asked to test out our new relationship and to see if we had actually grown from our mediation experience. The mediator apparently felt we were ready to handle this problem on our own, or else he would never have suggested this approach.

After heated but rational discussions, we negotiated the following solutions to the outstanding issues:

**For Myles:**

1. A maximum figure covering Karen's tax liability, to be paid quarterly, was established. There would be no pyramiding tax scale.
2. There would be no cost-of-living increase.
3. Beyond the agreed-to child support payments, Karen would be financially responsible for the children in all matters except their college education.
4. Myles would have a say in what camps the boys attended and in other outside activities.
5. Karen would be responsible for one half of the separation and divorce-related costs.

**For Karen:**

1. The new payment schedule would start January 1, 1982.
2. Karen would not be liable for any of Myles's debts.
3. Myles would carry $50,000 life insurance policies for each child, plus $100,000 for Karen.
4. There would be a very gradual scaling-down of the payments over the five-year period while Karen was preparing to support herself.

## The Tax Consultation Memorandum

After we reached this agreement, which to us seemed a major accomplishment, the tax consultant drew up a Tax Consultation Memorandum that contained his recommendations based on the new points we had just negotiated, plus what had previously been worked out and recorded as the Memorandum of Agreement. Copies of his recommendations went to Karen, Myles, and the mediator. Again, we were both offered the option of seeking independent financial advice.

## Discussion of Draft of Separation Memorandum

After all the steps were taken and the information sent to the mediator, he prepared a first draft of what would be the actual separation memorandum.

We arrived at the final session to go over this agreement paragraph by paragraph to be sure we understood everything. It was crucial to be sure that it represented exactly what we had agreed to.

We both showed up in a very tense mood. Despite the fact that we seemed to have everything worked out, we each figured the other had gone to an independent attorney and, as a result, would be armed with one last monkey wrench to throw the process into chaos again. It was one thing to negotiate, another to swallow all the uncertainty and accept that the agreement was complete. This agreement would soon be legal. It would soon become our guiding bill of rights (and responsibilities). This reality was still a little hard to accept.

The mediator quickly recognized our anxieties and just as quickly attempted to defuse them. His technique was to boost our confidence, pat us on the back, provide reassurance. We were acting almost like nervous children.

He began by reviewing our basic mediation goals: (1) to prepare us both for greater independence, and (2) to help us feel confident about our new situation.

He helped us minimize the tension by reviewing all the positive decisions we had made. Considering where we had started, those decisions represented major accomplishments.

The mediator continued by trying to put Myles more at ease, pointing out to him all the tax advantages that would be gained as a result of the settlement. He indicated that he felt that the settlement was fair, that it provided benefits for both while reflecting a reasonable level of compromise. He then turned to Karen and again showed how the agreement provided her with greater control over her life and greater responsibility for it than she had previously had. He emphasized that she should feel pleased about her participation in the mediation process and the results it already was helping to bring about. On this positive note, the final session began.

We reviewed the entire settlement agreement together and, surprisingly, found that we had no additional problems. We asked a few technical questions, but nothing of great importance. This discussion proceeded smoothly.

We were given a list of several independent attorneys who were familiar with divorce law and mediation. We agreed on one, who was then to receive a copy of our memorandum. He would rewrite it in such a way that it would serve as a legal separation agreement. At the appropriate time in the future, that agreement would become part of the divorce decree. It was clearly explained again that once we signed the agreement, we would be bound by its contents. We were advised once more by the mediator and the attorney that we could seek a review of the agreement by our own individual attorneys. Karen chose to do so, with the result that we were both confident that this agreement was the best possible for each of us.

## Mixed Emotions

We both experienced mixed emotions. On one hand, we experienced a great sense of relief that the ordeal was over. We were amazed at what we had accomplished; it was still hard to believe that we really had done it, and done it the way we had set out to do it. But we also felt sad. The accomplishment meant the end of a long relationship. Yet we were both proud of ourselves for doing something that we by now knew was necessary for our individual well-being. We had done it with the help of the mediator, but primarily by ourselves.

We left the mediator's office feeling numb. It didn't seem real. It was like awakening from a bad dream. We both also realized that a lot of our anger had dissipated, and we hoped that was a permanent condition. Lack of trust had been a major contributor to our anger; now we had tried to reestablish that trust through an intensive effort. It was a significant beginning following a significant end.

In the following days, we discussed the agreement and how we felt. We both felt good about the results. We did not feel the hostility and bitterness that we had seen in many of our friends who had been divorced using the traditional adversary approach. We had a sense of achievement, pride, and satisfaction with having taken an active role in stabilizing our lives after this major upheaval.

*Myles:* I felt that it was an equitable agreement. I was contributing financially to the care of the children, and I was returning the financial support to Karen that she had provided me while I was building a career. Now Karen was being given a similar opportunity to build her career while I provided the support. I had gone against all the advice of my friends and business associates, yet now I felt I had achieved what I had wanted to do.

*Karen:* I felt positive about finally gaining the confidence to stand up to Myles and, by doing that, to develop the tools to lead a life of my own. I was concerned about what would happen in the next few years, but felt confident that I had the capability and the stamina to deal with the major issues as they arose.

By pure coincidence, we signed our separation agreement on July 9, 1981, fourteen years to the day from when we were married.

CHAPTER 14

# What You Should Know About State Divorce Laws

**W**e have talked at length in the preceding chapters about things you might want to know before considering mediation. This might leave you worried that you are not knowledgeable enough or that you need to be a lawyer for mediation to work. This is not the case. It is true that some knowledge of the divorce laws in your area might be helpful in bolstering your confidence and in making you feel that your position in negotiation is tenable.

However, it is not necessary to have any specific legal knowledge at all. An integral part of mediation is the use of an advisory attorney who will provide all the legal information you need and will review the agreement prior to your signing it. It is also possible (just to make you feel you have left no stone unturned) to have an attorney of your choice serve as a consultant, giving you his opinion as to the degree of protection that the agreement offers you. This additional opinion is not a requirement, but it may help you feel more confident about your agreement. In addition, you may want to use the services of an accountant or a tax attorney if your situation is financially complicated or involves many mutual holdings. Getting adequate tax information may be critical to how you structure your settlement.

Even though it may appear that the use of specialists will escalate the cost and complicate the procedure, you will find that they will protect you in the long run. The added cost of advisory assistance is still considerably less than the cost of two opposing attorneys locked in a long court battle over the division of property.

With all these specialists, you may wonder why you need to know anything at all about state divorce laws. If you understand the legal framework within which you will be operating, you will be far less likely to have unrealizable expectations or to hold onto unrealistic negotiating positions. If fair offers are made, you will be able to recognize them as such.

If you have some knowledge of the property and custody laws of your state, you will be in for far fewer surprises during the divorce process. Some states automatically divide property by equal distribution, some by equitable distribution. These terms will prove critical in determining what you will get if you go to court. Knowing what they mean may help you in negotiating. Your state may have joint custody as a fixed arrangement in contested custody cases. If you know this before you begin, you can determine your strategy depending on whether you are hoping to gain joint custody or to prevent it. This kind of information enables you to determine how you can use mediation to meet your particular needs.

Since mediation provides you the opportunity to structure your own agreement, you can circumvent unpredictable or unwanted court decisions. If you familiarize yourself at all with adversary divorce rulings, you will be absolutely astonished by the unpredictable nature of the results. So much is left to a judge's discretion that you can never be really sure of how a case will be decided. If the judge has a punitive attitude toward the divorce, a case may end very differently than if she has a more open and progressive attitude. A judge's value system influences her decisions just as yours does, so you had better hope her values are similar to yours. If you don't want to be at the mercy of this kind of system, mediation will prove the way to sidestep it. And knowledge of the system and of the laws guiding it will help you make the choices that are in your own best interest.

## Some Definitions

**Custody**—or co-parenting as it is referred to in mediation, is an area in which some knowledge of the law may be helpful; however, remember that mediation allows the couple to form their own agreement regarding the parenting of their children as long as the agreement does not provide for something contrary to the best interest of the children. Under traditional law, the most common custody arrangement is sole custody. This involves one parent having the child live with him while the other parent has pre-arranged visitation rights. With sole custody, the custodial parent is responsible for the decision-making on all issues regarding the child. Generally, the child lives with the decision-making parent, and this parent has the right to take legal action if his decisions are not followed.

Joint custody—is an option in which both parents share the responsibilities and decision-making for the children. Joint custody attempts to give both parents an equal role in the child-rearing process, and it recognizes both parents as fit and equal to the task. Joint custody may be joint physically as well as legally. In joint physical custody, the children share their time equally with each parent. This may be done by equally dividing a week, a month, a year, or some other reasonable period of time. In other words, time-sharing is on a fifty/fifty basis. In joint legal custody, it is possible for the children to spend the majority of time with one parent while the legal rights and responsibilities are shared by both the parents.

Thirty-one states now allow joint custody as an acceptable arrangement. In joint custody arrangements, the daily decisions are generally made by whomever the child is actually with at that particular time. Major decisions, however, regarding health care, education, social interactions, and religious matters are reached by both parents. It is an arrangement that must be based on a strong level of cooperation between the parents.

Split custody—is the situation in which there is more than one child, and the parents agree that each of them will be responsible for one or more of the children. In effect, each parent has sole responsibility for a particular child or children and visitation rights for the remaining children.

## Some Questions
Who usually gets custody?—In the last few years there have been some changes in the area of custody awards. Traditionally, children, particularly if they were very young, were awarded to the mother under the "tender years" notion coupled with maternal preference standards—the courts believed that children belonged with their mothers.

In recent years, however, sex preferenced standards have been reduced and nonsexist or neutral standards have been substituted, stressing the "best interests of the child." Currently, more men are asking for and receiving sole custody of their children. While old patterns are slow to change and award patterns continue to favor the mother (in 90% of divorce cases mothers get custody of the children), an increasing number of women are finding it easier and more socially acceptable to voluntarily give up custody of children to the father. Nevertheless, the majority of fathers do not fight for custody, and so the majority of children following a divorce are likely to live with their mother.

If there is a court battle over custody, the judge has the final authority to make the decision. She will generally rely on the "best interest of the child" as a guideline. This is a subjective decision based on many variables and standards. Judges must make predictions and decisions about the two parents without really knowing either them or the children. They will rely on their own values and biases in reaching those decisions. The overburdened schedule they work under does not allow the luxury of time to deal with the psychological and emotional aspects of the divorce. Therefore, if you leave your custody decision in the hands of a court, you have absolutely no way to predict the outcome. Don't rely on rumors, and don't rely on friends or attorneys who tell you that "in this area the man (or the woman) always gets the children...." There is no formula. If you don't decide on your arrangement yourself, be prepared to take the risks.

**What is the role of children in discussions relating to custody?**—In mediation you and your spouse can determine what role you want your children to play. During the sessions on coparenting (custody) some couples may want to have their children present. Of course, that will depend on their age. If you feel that it will help your children understand what is happening concerning the separation and the arrangements for their future care, a session is planned with them, the parents and the mediator. Sometimes the mediator may want to have some time alone with the children to get to know them a little, and to help give them some understanding of the mediator's role. Under no circumstances should children be put in the position of having to choose one parent over the other. This responsibility can potentially be very damaging for everyone concerned. It is appropriate to listen to their thoughts about the situation if they are old enough to express them.

It is also appropriate to give them an opportunity to express their feelings. But the parents are still the decision-makers. They are the two people who are most familiar with their family as it has been and as they would like it to be. It is assumed that they will have the best interest of the children at heart as they plan their separation arrangements.

In the adversary system, children can be called in as witnesses to testify on custodial issues. The determination of whether or not the children will participate in this way is the prerogative of the courts and depends on the children's age, maturity, and particular situation.

**Rules about moving children out-or-state**—This issue can be worked out jointly, whether it relates to taking trips out of state or to establishing residence out-of-state. If cooperation and shared parenting are accepted, the fear of one spouse trying to disappear with the children will not exist. Consequently, out-of-state vacations should not pose a problem, since vacation-time will be prearranged and the spouse physically with the child has the right to decide where to go. If the issue is moving to another state, then the spouses will have to negotiate a coparenting (custody) arrangement such that the time is shared in some way that is acceptable to both parents and feasible for the children.

If an adversary relationship exists and the custodial parent takes the children out-of-state without the prior agreement of the noncustodial parent, then a contempt citation can be issued against the custodial parent. Similarly, if the noncustodial parent attempts to move out of state with the children without prearranged permission, the custodial parent can file a petition for contempt of court. In the latter case, the parent who initiates the unauthorized move could be in serious trouble for violation of the custody agreement. Either situation can be severely damaging to the children and can lead to more court costs and bitterness.

**Are custody arrangements final?**—In mediation, a couple always has the ability to bring an issue back to mediation at a later date if there is some change in the situation or if a conflict has arisen. Often, a clause is placed in the final agreement stating that the couple will return to mediation in the event of an unresolvable conflict. The other choice is to go to court to reopen the custody issue. This is an option available to both parties. Generally , a couple who has gone through mediation will have established a pattern of behavior that permits them to work out their problems themselves.

**Are children bound by the mediation agreement?**—Children who are minors are in essence bound to follow the arrangements agreed on by the adults. It is of course up to the parents to see that the children uphold the arrangements. If a child is vehemently against seeing one or the other of the parents, outside assistance might be advisable. Forcing children, whatever their age, is not advisable, and can often escalate rather than resolve a problem of this nature. The parents might want to consider getting the child, and perhaps the family, some help from a family therapist in identifying underlying issues.

There is also a need for both parents to be flexible about the children's schedules and sensitive about how those schedules affect the overall arrangements. As children get older, there will be an increasing number of social, athletic, and school events that will complicate the established schedule. These complications may cause children to resent the disruptions in their life. Mediation tends to reduce this as an issue because the parents are cooperating from the outset in making the best possible arrangements for the children.

**Can children have their own attorneys?**—In the adversary system, it is becoming more common for children to have attorneys representing them to ensure that their interests are heard. There are several states that appoint a guardian or lawyer to represent children's interests in difficult custody cases. This guardian or lawyer will inspect the child's living environment and will talk with the child and the parents independently. The guardian or lawyer can make recommendations to the court or to the couple's attorneys as to what are the best arrangements for the child. A great deal of weight is generally given to the recommendation by the children's attorney.

**How is child support determined?**—In mediation, support is based on the shared responsibility of both parents to provide the best conditions for the children. There are a variety of factors to be considered before an amount can be determined. Budgets are worked on and custody is determined before child support amounts are set. This order prevents either parent from using the children as "bargaining chips" in the negotiation sessions to get more money from the other spouse.

Factors considered in determining the amount of support include the following:

- Present income and future earning ability of each spouse,
- Assets and liabilities of each spouse,

- Needs of each spouse,
- Perceived effect on the standard of living that the children are accustomed to,
- Age and physical and emotional condition of the children to be supported,
- Long-term financial state of the children (whether or not they will receive inheritances, trusts or similar bequests),
- Need for special medical care or education for the children

After the spouses have worked through their budgets and reduced them to the essentials, support payments can be set based on who needs what. Mediation provides the couple with the flexibility to decide on figures they feel they can live with.

In the adversary system, court-ordered amounts vary considerably. There are "formulas"—such as that one child gets 20 percent of the husband's net income, and two children get 27 percent—but these formulas are just guidelines. Court-ordered payments hardly if ever cover all the needs of the children. And the custodial spouse, expecting enough child support for total care of the child, is likely to intensify what are probably impossible demands.

**How can I be sure support will be paid, and what can I do if it isn't?**— Mediation tends to ensure that payments will be made, because the paying spouse will have worked through the real uses to which money can be put. This helps relieve the sense that the spouse is paying to support the interests and life-style of the ex-spouse instead of the children. Also, having come to an agreement jointly fosters a commitment to follow through. In mediation, support is not thought of as a payment. It is viewed as part of total support—philosophical, emotional, and financial.

In mediation, if a problem should arise after the agreement is made (if, for example, the payments are not forthcoming), the couple can come back to mediation to reevaluate the situation. Lack of payments, however, is seldom an issue for couples who have completed mediation. In the adversary system or after mediation, if a spouse does not pay support, the other spouse can file a petition for contempt in the court where the decree was entered. Nonsupport actions can be taken either to divorce court or to criminal court.

The procedures often involve long delays before problems are resolved. The courts are overburdened, and the system for collection is complicated and limited in its powers. Noncompliance with support agreements has reached epidemic proportions. The difficulties imply that it is wise to avoid getting lost in the court maze if possible. "Attempting to collect child support from a determined or hostile ex spouse, can be a nightmare involving several trips to the courthouse accompanied each time by a lawyer and by the obligation to pay that lawyer."[1] If you jointly prepare your own agreement, you don't leave the paying spouse feeling used and prone to want to defeat the system that has ordered him to pay.

**Are child support and visitation linked?**—No matter which system is used, even if visitation is withheld, support payments must still be made. Custody payments are considered totally separate from visitation rights. On the other hand, visitation rights may not be denied even if support payments are not continued. If either support or visitation agreements are not being met, a spouse can file a petition for contempt with the divorce or criminal court. In mediation all aspects of parenting are inevitably linked. The family is restructured, but the parenting must go on. It is very unlikely that parents working in an atmosphere of cooperation will resort to the "games" often played by divorcing couples under the adversary system. Withholding support payments or denying visitation are power plays that show up in mediation too, but the mediator has the tools to help the couple offset them. The best interest of the children is certainly not served by competitive and self-centered behavior. Parents who have successfully completed mediation will generally not engage in these tactics.

**If I am not legally divorced can I get child support?**—The end product of mediation is a memorandum of agreement. This is not a legal document unless it is drafted into a legal separation agreement. When a legal separation has been signed by all the necessary people (both partners, the attorney, and a witness) and is notarized, then the support and visitation arrangements go into effect. Both parties are bound to uphold the provisions of the agreement, even if it is never turned into a divorce.

There are several states that will allow a person to file for custody and support of the children without filing for separation or divorce. You would need to get further information on which states allow this and to find out about the ramifications of taking that approach.

**Can child support payments be changed?**—If significant changes occur in the financial circumstances within a family—for example, if one spouse invents something and becomes very wealthy, or if a spouse is laid off from a job and his income is severely reduced or completely stopped—then the couple can come back to mediation and renegotiate their support arrangements. Of course the couple also has the adversary option of going to court, but this course of action can be risky because no one has any way of knowing whether the current award won't get reduced instead of increased.

**What are the tax implications of child support payments?**—If, as is most often the case, the father is paying the child support, he will need to know that child support is not deductible from his taxable income. It is also not taxable income to the spouse receiving the payments. Alimony (spousal support), on the other hand, is deductible by the one who is paying, and is taxable to the one who is receiving.

There is a method called "Lesterizing" whereby the child support and alimony are combined into one figure. This is most useful when there is a large disparity between the incomes of the two people—where one is the only wage earner and one has been staying home caring for the children. Under this procedure, payments are considered to be combined, so that the total amount is deductible by the spouse making the payments and taxable to the one receiving the payments. This approach creates additional disposable income by minimizing tax liability.

All these tax considerations are reviewed and analyzed with a couple during the appropriate sessions. If a couple has a very high income with a more complicated tax situation, an accountant or tax attorney may be brought in for assistance at the appropriate time during the mediation process. These same considerations can be made a part of mediation or a part of an adversary process; however, the structure of mediation establishes a point during the negotiations when these issues must be considered.

**How can I be assured that my children are getting the things they need from the money I am paying?**— Once again, mediation fosters trust in the other spouse's ability as a fit an caring parent. When you work out budgets in the course of mediation, you will see how much money is needed for the essentials and where this money should go to meet the children's needs. Also, since both parents share a close relationship with the child, it will be apparent to you if the child is not receiving the necessities you have agreed to provide. At that time, you or the other spouse can communicate your concerns regarding the needs of the children and reevaluate whether there is money available that is not being appropriately used, or whether unusual constraints have interfered with the normal financial situation. In extreme cases of intransigence on the part of the spouse receiving payments, reliance on the courts is available as a last resort.

## Laws and Issues Relating to Alimony Payments

In mediation, alimony like child support is based on identified need. A major goal of mediation is to gradually decrease the dependency of one spouse on the other. Consequently, spousal support (alimony) is generally limited to the time it would take for the dependent spouse to establish financial independence, whether through job training and education or through some other clearly defined steps. The amount of payments is determined on the basis of what the budgeting sessions determined to be the needs. The amount is agreed on by the couple, as is the period during which it will be paid. Payments may be higher the first few years and diminish as the dependent spouse becomes more financially secure.

As with child support, there is no fixed amount or formula you can count on if you go to court. The amount awarded may be anywhere from near zero to 50 percent of the other spouse's income. The judge is also likely to consider the ability of the spouse seeking the support to support himself.

Women are getting less support now than in the past. Courts are not likely to burden a husband with support of an ex-wife until she remarries or dies. Unless there are extenuating circumstances, such as handicaps, children at home that require special care, or other special needs, it is expected that most women will work and eventually support themselves.

**How are alimony payments enforced?**—Like child support, alimony is worked out jointly in mediation; as a result, enforcing the payments is not generally a source of trouble.

If there have been changes in the circumstances, the couple can return to mediation and renegotiate the agreement. The couple can also go to court if the nonadversary route fails.

**Does one spouse always get alimony?**—No. In mediation it is not uncommon for couples to find that, because of equality of earning power, there is no need for alimony. If the court system is used, there is no set answer as to whether there will be any alimony award, who will get it, and how much that person will receive.

**What if the spouse receiving alimony gets remarried?**—Generally, if a spouse receiving alimony remarries, the alimony will end. Many states have laws that hold that alimony ends on remarriage. If the couple has worked out a Lester Agreement, combining alimony and child support, a percentage of the money will have been indicated as spousal support, and the monthly payment will be reduced by that amount.

**Can only women receive alimony?**—No. Alimony can be awarded to either spouse depending on the income and circumstances of the couple. In mediation, the couple works through individual budgets before determining who needs what amount, what current and future career opportunities each spouse has, and the ability of the spouse with greater financial resources to pay support. Amounts are then agreed on jointly.

**Can the amount be changed in the future?**—Mediation allows for almost any issue to be renegotiated if significant changes in circumstances occur. Sometimes a de-escalation clause is included in the agreement to cover what happens if a spouse loses his job or has a severe decline in income for unforeseen reasons. Also, if a spouse's income increases drastically, it is possible to renegotiate an agreement. Cost-of-living increases and adjustments in payment to result from expected changes in financial situation can be written into the agreement.

## Tax Laws Regarding Alimony

Alimony is deductible by the payer and taxable to the recipient. It is crucial to the person paying that he have a written agreement, whether it is a decree of divorce or a decree of separation, in order for the alimony payments to be deductible. A verbal, voluntary, or informal agreement to support a spouse will not suffice to designate payments as alimony.

Expenses of the dependent spouse for home mortgages, medical expenses, and life insurance premiums may affect tax and alimony. Payments for these expenses may be made directly to the responsible companies rather than directly to the dependent spouse, but they may still not be considered alimony. There are a variety of contingencies regarding these issues; an accountant would need to review your particular situation to determine the best arrangement.

The amount of support to the spouse and the minor children can be combined so that the entire amount is deductible to the husband and taxable to the wife. If this is done, a larger amount than can be given to the dependent spouse to cover the cost of the taxes. Both parties benefit from the larger amount of disposable income available to the family as a whole.

## Marital Property

**What items are considered joint property, and what is considered sole property?**—Marital property (property that is jointly owned) is all the material things that a couple has acquired (whether by one or both parties) during the course of their marriage without regard to title. Both spouses are considered to have contributed, and therefore both are entitled to a fair share of the items. Included are inheritances or gifts that have been given to both spouses (as a couple) as well as items they have purchased or accumulated jointly. Pensions and retirement funds contributed to during the course of a marriage are also marital property.

Sole property is what belongs to only one person and can include:

- Inheritances.
- Property or material goods owned or acquired before the marriage.
- Gifts.
- Property bought with money that was inherited or received as a gift.
- Property exchanged for property that was inherited as a gift.
- Property excluded from marital property by a valid agreement.
- Increases in value of property that is not marital property and has not been improved in any way by the owner (passive owner). The increase is clearly the result of increases in market value, the economy, or inflation.
- Property acquired after the legal separation or divorce.

**What are the tax implications?**—While a critical factor in dividing the marital property is the needs of the parties, it is possible that the tax ramifications can be minimized by the way in which property transfers are structured. There are ways by which an equal division of jointly owned property will not be a taxable event, and will therefore result in no additional tax liabilities.

The impact of taxes on settlements is complex, and a tax advisor can help determine the effects of particular state laws on marital property settlements. Hopefully, some of the complicated tax problems will soon be diminished. A bill is currently in Congress that, if passed, eliminates the tax burden incurred when property changes hands during divorce.

**How is property distributed?**—In mediation, the last step in property settlements is property division. This occurs after the the identification and evaluation of property has been completed. Some division is worked out by the couple on their own, either before the mediation sessions begin or during the mediation. In general, the starting point in mediation is a fifty/fifty division of marital property; the couple adjust this proportion until they have worked out an arrangement they feel is equitable for them.

Equitable and equal are not the same. Equitable involves working out an arrangement that allows for a division of property based on the contribution of each spouse to the marriage. This includes the partner who may have worked as a homemaker and earned considerably less than the other spouse. It is also affected by the economic circumstances of each spouse, as well as by what each spouse has as sole property. Pensions and future earnings are taken into account as divisible property. Percentages can be applied to the time the pension plan was in effect before the couple were married, to determine the portion due the other spouse.

In mediation, there are options available to a couple as to the division of their property. Sometimes arrangements are worked out based on a trade-off of assets, and sometimes future contributions are balanced against present ones. All arrangements are unique to the couple.

Some states, such as California, have community property laws that require fifty/fifty splits. A few states are title states: in these states, a person gets or shares things only if his name appears on the title. It is useful to know which property distribution formula your state uses; this knowledge may influence your bargaining strategy.

**How is the value of property determined?**—The value of property such as jewelry or artwork can be determined using an appraiser, or by checking the appraised value of the items on your insurance policy, if that appraisal is fairly recent. In the case of a house, two independent real estate agents can be called in to tell each spouse what the fair market value of the house would be. Cars can be taken to a car dealer for an estimate of the current value, or the Blue Book can be checked by either spouse. Many savings and loan associations will have a copy of the Blue Book available.

In mediation, evaluation time is thought of as an opportunity to have a couple begin to work cooperatively. The mediator will try to use what the couple already knows about their property and possessions, and will encourage them to work out the tasks necessary to find out the value of their property. Marital property is valued from the date of the first mediation session. A pension attorney, accountant, or actuary may be consulted for information about pensions and retirement funds, so that the couple can figure out the present value and the contribution made by the spouse, and the percent that is due to the other spouse as part of the property settlement. Tax shelters, too, have worth. You will probably need a recognized authority to set their value even though they generate no money.

**How can I be sure that all assets are disclosed?**—The mediation process bases a great deal of its success on trust between the two persons participating. However, a clause or Warranty of Full Disclosure can be included in the legal separation agreement. It states that if a party discovers some asset that had been hidden, there is legal recourse against the dishonest party. This warranty can be worded in several different ways, but it may include a clause entitling the person who discovers a hidden asset to that asset in its entirety. Or it may state that the person owning the property not admitted to at the time of the agreement will pay the other spouse one-half of the fair market value of that item.

**Legal discovery procedures**—In the adversary system, it is very possible for a spouse to get away with concealing assets, because there is little opportunity for the two people involved to interact and discover such omissions.

In the adversary system, lawyers can use both formal and informal discovery techniques. Sometimes the lawyers simply exchange information about clients informally. This is information they know they would have to provide under any circumstances; obtaining information this way is not unusual. In a formal discovery process, a record of the facts is established; the future agreement is based on these facts. This record provides a check against misrepresentation and can be used as the basis for a judge reconsidering a judgment. The more complicated a case is and the more distrust is involved, the more formal the discovery process has to be.

**How are long-term investments and debts handled?**—During the mediation session on division of property, a couple works out how they want to deal with long-term investments and debts. If a significant loss would be involved in liquidating long-term investments, it is possible to make trade-offs so that one spouse could keep these assets, and provide the other spouse with something of equal value. If there are not sufficient assets to make those trade-offs, other options may be considered such as a percentage to be obtained by both at a future date. After researching how much would have to be invested currently in a similar plan to reach the same result at maturity, one spouse will invest money in an investment that will have an equal return at some future date. Sometimes, because of the need to support two households instead of one, and because of the unavailability of resources, long-term investments have to be liquidated even at a loss of potential value.

Part of the work a couple does in mediation is to explore all possible options and avenues they can think of that could help them manage their changing lives. The court system's inability to provide this flexibility, often leads to an unnecessary loss of funds.

**Under what circumstances does the dependent spouse share in the supporting spouse's future income or business?**—This is an issue currently getting a lot of attention. In California, a case relating to this subject is now pending. In mediation, this question can be negotiated. Often one spouse has contributed many years of work, while the other spouse continued his education and obtained degrees that will enable him to have a high income in the future.

Working out an arrangement in mediation regarding future value of professional degrees will save a couple from a potentially costly court battle. Spouses have recently been awarded percentages of medical practices and money for future years based on predicted earnings of the other spouse. Once again, there is no formula for responding to this issue and no guarantee that the court will see fit to award a spouse anything at all that is based on future earnings.

## The Laws in Your State

There are different laws in different states. You should try to be as familiar as possible with those that apply to you. It takes time and some assistance, but it can be done. The questions in this chapter provide guidance, but they are not exhaustive.

A key point to remember is that under mediation any point can be dealt with in a structured way; although you have no formula for predicting how the settlement goes, you at least have the opportunity and tools to help frame the settlement. The adversary process limits your role in formulating solutions and tends to be unpredictable.

There are several steps that you could take to find out as much as you can about the divorce laws applicable where you live, and the patterns that have been established in settling the issues you will have to face:

1. Look up the legal statutes pertaining to divorce. These can be found in law libraries, court or bar association libraries, law school and university libraries, and even in local public libraries.

2. If you have friends or relatives who are lawyers, contact them and see if they can provide you with the proper written materials, or with leads to help you find them.

3. Locate a mediator in your area, using the steps outlined in Chapter 6. Mediators can help guide you to the information you need.

4. Contact your local bar association. They can put you in touch with an independent attorney who can help you find this information and who may be willing to help interpret it.

5. If you feel the experience would be worthwhile, contact your attorney or an attorney acquaintance and see if it is possible for you to attend a contested and an uncontested divorce hearing. Experiencing the reality may help you decide what to do.

6. Read over some divorce decisions, but be advised that reading specific cases may be misleading. Each case is open to varied interpretations depending on the situation; you cannot make predictions on the basis of other people's cases.

Educating yourself about the divorce laws that pertain to your situation can be time-consuming, but it can also be very useful. Knowledge of the system helps take away some of the uncertainty. You won't have all the answers, but you will feel less bewildered and more confident as you proceed.

# CHAPTER 15

# Post Mediation

## Completing the Divorce Procedure

Marital mediation is a structured process that adheres to a set of basic guidelines. However, there is considerable flexibility within the structure: each family situation is unique and is treated independently. In our case, it took about four months to finish the process and sign the memorandum of agreement. The delay was due to our own scheduling problems, previous business commitments, and some purposeful dawdling.

After signing our memorandum of agreement, we were to take it to an independent advisory attorney. We were given a list of several who were familiar with mediation and its goals, and who would therefore not attempt to undermine what we had accomplished. We chose one, and we both set up an appointment to review the document. The advisory attorney reviewed the agreement with us and asked if we had any additions, questions, or problems. After our brief meeting, he told us that he would prepare our legal separation agreement. He would send each of us a copy for our review. If any further questions arose, or corrections had to be made, we were to contact him.

In a few weeks, copies of the formal document were sent to both of us. In addition, to all the issues we had negotiated, he had added paragraphs protecting both of us—paragraphs standard in such agreements.

We both reviewed the agreement and found a few minor changes that were necessary. We contacted him, the adjustments were made, and the agreement was finally ready to be signed. At this time we were again offered the option of seeking independent counsel not associated with the mediation process for one final review. It was our last chance to make sure that we knew what we were signing and that there were no remaining problems. Karen sought a final review by an attorney, and was told that the agreement was both reasonable and fair and that it would hold up in court. We were both ready to sign.

## We Sign the Agreement

By the end of the summer of 1981, we met once again with our independent attorney who had drafted the agreement. We each spent a few minutes alone with him. During this time, he carefully reviewed the agreement with us and then we both signed it, witnessed by a notary public. It thus became an official legal separation agreement.

Then the real cooperation had to start. We had to begin to execute the agreement. Though it was often tedious and at times uncomfortable, we had both agreed to a settlement and this made the actual implementing of the requirements a lot easier to cope with. Neither one of us expressed bitterness or anger, and we seemed to be able to get along with each other more comfortably than we had in a very long time.

There was about one and a half years between the time we signed the legal separation and the actual filing for the divorce. This again was a result of our own situation and not a function of the settlement. We were both satisfied with the agreement; neither one of us wanted to redo it. Even more important, we were satisfied with the process we had used to generate that agreement. No further issues arose during the interval that in any way delayed the final step of filing for a divorce.

We had both been through a lot emotionally. Neither one was involved with anyone else. No remarriage was imminent. There was no rush to finalize the divorce. Part of the delay was a conscious decision to wait, let what we had done sink in, be sure it was what we both wanted, and then go ahead and complete the process.

## We File for Divorce

As time went by it was apparent that there was no reason not to file for divorce. There was no chance of reconciliation, and so we made the decision to finalize the divorce. It was time to move on. In addition, all the positive tax advantages, especially those for Myles that had been worked out, required that the actual divorce take place. In the fall of 1982, Myles's accountant advised him that he would suffer financial consequences at tax time if he did not finalize the divorce before the end of the year.

The final steps began when an attorney was contacted to represent one of us and file for the divorce. It is standard procedure for one person to sue the other for divorce. We decided that Myles would sue for a no-fault divorce on the grounds of incompatibility. The attorney understood that we had mediated our separation agreement and that we were working together even though he was representing only Myles for this legal action.

*Myles:* I was nervous about Karen's being served with the papers by the county sheriff (again, standard procedure). I didn't know how she would react to that. Although we had decided that I would be the one to sue, I thought that she might panic when the papers got delivered to her in person by a sheriff. The attorney had sent a letter informing her that this would be happening, but I couldn't be sure that she had read the letter or had paid much attention to it. When Karen did receive the papers, she was supposed to sign them in the presence of a notary. When I didn't hear anything from the attorney for several weeks, I began to get nervous. I wasn't sure what the delay was. Karen, as it turns out, had just taken her time about taking care of the paperwork. She didn't feel as much pressure as I did to get things completed. I needed to have the divorce by January 1 to get the tax advantages the divorced status would provide.

## The Divorce Hearing

Finally the attorney did receive the signed documents and set a hearing for the middle of December. The hearing was to take place before a magistrate of the court. I was required to be there, with a witness and my attorney. The court stenographer would also be present. Karen was not required to appear, but she chose to attend. When she arrived at the hearing accompanied by a young woman, I became anxious. I was sure trouble was brewing. Was this an attorney? Was there going to be a battle after all?

*Karen:* Myles had been all agitated for the last month or so about the rush to get the divorce completed. He had a lot more at stake in terms of tax payments than I did. Myles has always lived under the tyranny of time. He adheres to rigid schedules and has little patience. I assured him that everything was getting done and would be completed on time. All the necessary papers were signed and delivered as promised. Even though I was not required to attend the divorce hearing, I decided that I didn't want this event to go by without my participation. I had been a part of everything so far—why not this last step?

At the last moment, I decided that I didn't want to be totally alone at the hearing. I called a very close friend who had been through her own divorce, and asked her to go with me for moral support. Having her there really helped.

The magistrate got right to the point. Myles's attorney was to present the case. Then Myles was asked routine questions about what county he lived in and how long he had lived apart from Karen. The witness was asked to corroborate the facts. The magistrate explained the procedure and rights of each person. He then spoke privately with Karen since she was not represented by counsel. He wanted to be sure that she understood that she did have the right to counsel and that she was there voluntarily and was not contesting anything within the agreement.

When the facts of the agreement were verified, the hearing ended. The magistrate indicated that, since the details of the previously signed agreement were all worked out, he saw no reason to question them further. He would present the document to the judge for approval as soon as possible.

Two weeks later, the divorce was granted. We were notified that the official date of our divorce was December 27, 1982.

## We Look Back

*Myles:* It was extremely difficult for me to leave Karen and my children, and then to initiate the final steps toward dissolving the marriage. From my point of view, the reason it took so long to finish it was because I had no animosity toward Karen. I wasn't bitter or angry at her. I felt bad about our situation. I knew I had caused her pain and unhappiness by insisting on getting divorced. I felt bad for my children, because they would now be part of a broken home. Certain opportunities and experiences I felt they should have, they might never have—at least not with me. Maybe that wouldn't be apparent to them.

I knew something was wrong with our marriage. I didn't think we could fix it. I couldn't see living together just for the children. It had to end. Until I heard of mediation, however, I felt my only option was through the courts. In my mind courts were synonymous with distrust anger, hostility, bitterness, unresolved hatred, and revenge—a collection of demons straight from Pandora's Box. I didn't harbor these emotions. I cared about Karen and her feelings. I loved my children. I couldn't see getting involved in a process that would alienate me from my children and widen the gap between Karen and me.

In this respect mediation afforded me the opportunity to resolve an inner conflict as well as the conflict between Karen and me. Without this option it seemed to me then, and still seems to me now, that these issues could never have been worked out. The thought of going to court was out of the question. Karen and I and the children would probably have continued together until we had destroyed each other.

I had taken an action I never would have believed was possible for me when I initiated the divorce, but I still had to be able to face myself in the mirror every morning. If I couldn't find a way to neutralize my guilt and end my self-recrimination, what kind of life would I be able to lead? Mediation was a way to ease my conscience and give me an opportunity to work out a very fair agreement of which I could be proud.

As far as I am concerned, the settlement we worked out was fair to all of us. I know how much money we had together as well as how much income I was earning. I knew what my limits were and I had my idea of what was fair. I am not ashamed to face myself and I feel good about what we accomplished by working together.

After it was over, I thought of what might have happened if we had opted for the adversary approach. I figured that in our situation, three scenarios could have unfolded when it came to the financial aspects of our agreement. First, it could have evolved into something similar to what we generated through mediation. Second, Karen could have gotten what she might consider a "better deal." Finally I could have gotten the better deal.

No matter how it turned out, we wouldn't have been able to participate in the decision-making process ourselves. We probably would have been told not to trust each other or talk to each other. We would have drifted further apart, become hostile and uncooperative. We knew that we would continue to have contact because of the children as well as family and some friends we still shared. What possible advantage could the adversary process have offered us? It seems to me it offered nothing positive at all.

What if Karen had gotten more from me? What if I had been able to get away with giving her less? One of us would certainly have remained angry. What good would that have done? I'm certain that because of mediation, Karen and I communicate with each other more effectively than when we were married, and the chief beneficiaries of that improvement are the children. Growing up is not easy, whether one's parents are together or divorced. Divorce adds its own stress. If the parents can still talk to each other and support each other with respect to the children, then the impact of divorce can be minimized. I know that while I am not physically present as much as I would like to be, my input into their lives is nearly as much as it would have been if Karen and I had remained together. This wouldn't be possible without the sense of cooperation as parents that the mediation process instilled in us.

During the sessions, there were a lot of things that Karen and I were able to say to each other that we had never said before. I think the expression of some of those feelings enabled each of us to finish our past relationship and start anew with a different perspective on each other. I have grown to respect Karen and I would hope she feels the same toward me. Mediation has enabled us to develop a friendship, despite our past history and present circumstances.

We have both come out of our divorce with something to be proud of. When I married Karen, I thought it was "until death do us part." Things changed. At least I can say I'm proud of myself and Karen for how we handled it. Without a doubt it is because of mediation that I can go on with my life independently and feel good about myself.

*Karen:* After the fact, there are always questions. I've wondered how things would have turned out if I had used the adversary system. There are days when I'm feeling sorry for myself for one reason or another, and I question whether I could have gotten more money, more concessions from Myles, if I had gone to court. I guess nobody ever feels they got everything they wanted or is thrilled with their settlement. However, I have learned it is possible to achieve a settlement both people can live with. I realize that, although I am certainly not in the financial position I was in before my divorce, that is inherent in the situation.

All in all, there were many positives in the divorce process for me. In many ways, mediation changed my life. If I had chosen to use the adversary system, I'm not sure how I would have managed after the divorce. All my married life I had been a shadow behind Myles. If a lawyer had stood up for me, talked for me, substituted for me, I would have gone right on being a shadow. When the divorce process was over, I would have been no better, and perhaps a lot worse, off. The lawyer would be long gone, Myles would be gone, and I would have been left, just as I was the day he moved out—standing in the kitchen crying. I would still have been unable to decide whether to put my right or left foot down first—no direction, no decision-making capability—just alone....

Friends and family who knew me before my separation and mediation can attest to the fact that I was probably one of the least assertive persons they knew. At a party I would practically disappear into the scenery, clinging helplessly to Myles. I had no identity other than as Myles's wife or as my children's mother. When I came to those first mediation sessions, I was so scared and so lacking in self-confidence that I'm still surprised that I didn't totally disintegrate. I still can't comprehend that those few short sessions could give me the courage and conviction to be "just me."

Those small steps, the subtle confirmation by the mediator that my positions and points had validity gave me the little proofs I needed to begin to reestablish my self image. Stepping out of the protected environment of daughter-wife was so totally unknown to me that I don't think I had ever made a statement that I hadn't looked to a man to corroborate. In mediation I had to speak for myself—no small task. Bit by bit the safe environment of mediation allowed me to open up. I did have thoughts and feelings about the issues that would affect the rest of my life, and here was a place I could express them without fear. Facing Myles directly in the mediation arena wasn't as threatening or intimidating as it used to be. Having an equal opportunity to speak without his interrupting me, yelling at me, or having a tantrum gave me a good feeling. Little by little we learned to hear each other, maybe for the first time.

During our sessions, I began to be able to face the future more clearly. Working out my support caused me to rethink my career goals. The fact that support doesn't go on indefinitely at first nearly scared me to death. By the end of the sessions I was almost ready to tell Myles I could manage on my own—I felt I could almost tell him to keep all his money, I could get on with my life without his help. The mediator guided me in reaching a balance so that I would be provided the money I would need to go back to school. I realize now that, had support been paid to me for life, I probably would not have had the incentive to return to school, and I would not have pushed myself to achieve the graduate degree I wanted and needed.

Mediation makes you think. It makes you speak and feel and participate. You can't sit back and just observe—there is no one else to take over for you. I feel as though I sort of slithered into mediation on my belly, and come out walking upright for the first time in my life. Myles and I are probably better friends now than we ever were. We stopped seeing each other in our roles and began to see each other as people. Because we didn't turn our divorce into a war, we aren't enemies. Our children have had a relatively easy adjustment, because we have maintained a respect for each other as individuals.

Learning how to deal directly with each other in mediation has made it possible for us to work out the problems that have come up since our divorce. Even though I have sole custody, we discuss major issues and try to make joint decisions.

I believe that Myles gained a respect for me as a result of mediation that perhaps he never had. I suspect that he thought I would whine and cry and give in on all counts to his demands. I kind of expected that myself. Somehow mediation gave us both a new way of looking at ourselves and at each other. It also helped us to be able to look at our marriage and not feel that we had wasted so many years in vain: there had been many valuable aspects to our relationship.

I would advise any woman to consider mediation as a separation or divorce procedure. It is a growth experience that you do not get in the adversary system, an opportunity to begin shaping your own life. In a divorce you will ultimately be left on your own, whether you want it or not, so try to be as ready as you can. Help yourself by taking some responsibility for your own actions. Overcome the fear; step out of the mold. It isn't easy, but there are no easy answers. If I had to make the choice again, I would do it exactly the same way. I feel as though I have saved myself from years of wasting energy on hate, bitterness, and vengeance. I have much more positive things to do with my life than dwell on past hurts and faults. Mediation looks not to the past, but to the future.

CHAPTER 16

# The Future
# Of Mediation

## Winning
## At a Losing
## Game

**D**ivorce has never been approved of by society. In the not-so distant past, if a couple wanted to dissolve their marriage, they needed to be wealthy, extremely persistent, and strong enough to handle the resulting disapproval of those around them.

The legal system has mirrored society's outlook on separation and divorce. The system has made divorce difficult if not impossible, and often embarrassing. Yet the adversary system is still the usual way to dissolve a marriage. It is an overburdened and outdated system.

One brief but important example of the failure of the adversary system is the deplorable situation with regard to child support. As recently as November 23, 1983, Judy Mann in her column in the *Washington Post* described the plight of the "hundreds of thousands of families headed by women who have been plunged into poverty by divorce."[1] She states that defaults on payment of child support cheated children out of approximately four billion dollars in 1981 alone. The adversary system imposes financial decisions on divorcing couples; these decisions are not being upheld. What is happening to divorced families has become a national disgrace directly attributable to the inability of the adversary system to enforce its decisions.

The democratic system has always relied on its populace to uphold its laws through cooperation and respect. Where would our system of taxation be, for example, if that cooperation did not generally exist? When that cooperation breaks down, the courts become severely overloaded. That is what has happened with respect to enforcement of our divorce laws. A lack of respect has developed for the system's ability to uphold the law. A process of rebuilding that respect is necessary if the problems of divorced couples are to be solved. A change in the system is long overdue.

## Changing Trends

Many lawyers and judges are beginning to realize what an impossible task has been thrust on them. They are overwhelmed with new cases as the divorce rate rises and bogged down by cases already in litigation. They are becoming frustrated and, as a result, more outspoken against the old approach. They too are looking for a better way. The trend is toward using the techniques of mediation, conciliation and arbitration to handle divorce and other domestic disputes.

The time has come to reexamine the process of divorce and the monopoly the legal profession has had over that process. Marital mediation is a real alternative for couples who find themselves contemplating separation and divorce, and also for couples already divorced who are looking for a way to resolve nagging controversies left unresolved by the adversary process. Mediation does not remove the pain and the problems, but it recognizes that they exist and that a solution must deal with them.

Mediation can help to bring about that change. It is a humane and constructive process that leaves the people involved with a new sense of dignity and reason to uphold the decisions which they have reached together. Family structure is in transition, and divorce is a fact of life. Mediation cannot solve the problems that led a couple to the decision to seek a divorce, but it can help that couple accomplish that divorce in a compassionate and constructive way. A couple's relationship is restructured, not destroyed.

It has become apparent that the adversary system is unable to provide the kind of emotional support a couple needs during divorce. For that reason, the trend is to take divorce issues out of the hands of the courts whenever possible and return them to the control of those most directly involved—the couples themselves. In more and more instances, states are encouraging and often requiring mediation in custody and property cases. Attorneys and judges are suggesting that couples mediate rather than litigate. At some point in the not too distant future, it is entirely possible that the majority of divorces will be worked out by the families themselves with the help of a neutral third party. Lawyers and judges will then serve as consultants and advisors rather than as spokespersons and decisionmakers.

The people who have been involved in mediation until now are pioneers. "Eighty years ago, only the rich dared to divorce. Now the affluent and the educated seek divorce mediation; perhaps eighty years hence, most divorces will be mediated."[2]

**Attorneys and Mediation**—Attorneys have felt the tide turning away from the adversary system. It is now common for attorneys to encourage clients to mediate and to call on the resources of tax consultants, accountants, or actuaries to help couples arrive at solutions without litigation.

In many respects, the divorce lawyer is only a servant of an ineffective system. We are sure that there are many practicing attorneys who feel a responsibility to support the best interests of the family, but who sometimes feel confounded by their duty to represent only the interests of their client. We feel that for the most part they too will welcome mediation. Perhaps they may even become its strongest supporters.

A large number of people currently taking mediation training are attorneys. The legal profession has a crucial role to play in the arena of divorce. The most frequently cited reason for a couple's choosing mediation is that they have been referred by their attorney. With the support of the legal profession, mediation will be accepted far more rapidly as a viable alternative.

## The Future of Mediation
As for the future, it is clear that divorce mediation is gaining legislative as well as popular support. Court-mandated custody mediation is no longer a rarity. In some states, such as California, courts require mediation for all couples with children under 12 who have custody and visitation disputes. In Chicago, mediation became mandatory in contested cases on January 1, 1983, making it a requirement that divorcing parents participate in three two-hour sessions to help facilitate agreements outside the courtroom. Legislatures in many more states are in the process of adopting procedures to require mediation in child custody cases.

Conciliation courts and mediation services, both public and private, are being established throughout the country. Couples like ourselves who have survived divorce relatively unscathed are becoming more common.

Despite all the publicity on contested divorce, less than 10 percent actually reach the courts. This means that almost all divorce cases are settled through negotiations between attorneys. Why not negotiate for yourself? We believe that the only reason mediation is not being used as a primary means of reaching a separation agreement is because people are not aware that it exists. We believe that people would consider and try it if they understood what it could do for them.

Mediation will work in almost all situations if given a chance. We believe that in the future, mediation will be the usual method for the dissolution of a marriage. It is with this hope that we have written our book and told our story. We wanted to provide the information to let people judge for themselves.

We weren't special, unusual, or particularly courageous. We saw a chance to make something positive out of a painful situation. It worked for us—it can work for you. Mediation is a way to achieve divorce with dignity.

# FOOTNOTES

Chapter 2
[1]Weiss, Robert S. *Marital Separation*. New York: Basic Books, 1975, p. 265.

Chapter 6
[1]Meroney, Anne E. Mediation and Arbitration of Separation and Divorce Agreements. *Wake Forest Law Review*. 15,4 (August 1979), p. 472.

Chapter 8
[1]Deutsch, Morton. *The Resolution of Conflict*. New Haven: Yale University Press, 1973, p. 17.
[2]Fisher, Roger and Ury, William. *Getting to Yes*. Boston: Houghton Mifflin, 1981, p. 33.

Chapter 14
[1]Carrod, David Clayton. A Modest Proposal to End our National Disgrace. *The Family Advocate*. 30 (1979), p. 31.

Chapter 16
[1]Mann, Judy. "Child Support." *The Washington Post*, November 23, 1983, p. C1.
[2]Winks, Patricia L. Divorce Mediation: A Nonadversary Procedure for the No-Fault Divorce. *Journal of Family Law*. 19 (August 1981), p. 650.

# BIBLIOGRAPHY

## I. Books

1 Cohen, Herb. *You Can Negotiate Anything.* New York: Bantam Books, 1980.

2 Coogler, O.J. *Structured Mediation in Divorce Settlement: A Handbook for Marital Mediation.* Lexington, Massachusetts: Lexington Books, 1978.

3 Coulson, Robert. *Fighting Fair.* New York: The Free Press, 1983.

4 Divorce Mediation Research Project. *Directory of Mediation Services 1982.* Denver: Divorce Mediation Research Project, 1982.

5 Filley, Alan C. *Interpersonal Conflict Resolution.* Glenville, Illinois: Scott, Foresman and Company, 1975.

6 Fisher, Roger, and Ury, William. *Getting to Yes.* Boston: Houghton Mifflin Company, 1981.

7 Friedman, James T. *The Divorce Handbook.* New York: Random House, 1982.

8 Gettleman, Susan, and Markowitz, Janet. *The Courage to Divorce.* New York: Simon and Schuster, 1974.

9 Haynes, John M. *Divorce Mediation: A Practical Guide for Therapists and Counselors.* New York: Springer, 1981.

10 Krantzler, Mel. *Creative Divorce.* New York: M. Evans and Company, Inc., 1973.

11 Mitchelson, Marvin. *Made in Heaven, Settled in Court.* Los Angeles: J.P. Tarcher, Inc., 1976.

12 Ricci, Isolina. *Mom's House, Dad's House.* New York: Macmillan Publishing Co., Inc., 1980.

13 Roman, Mel, and Haddad, William. *The Disposable Parent: The Case for Joint Custody.* New York: Penguin Books, 1978.

14 Salk, Dr. Lee. *What Every Child Would Like Parents to Know about Divorce.* New York: Harper and Row, 1978.

15 Wallerstein, Judith S., and Kelly, Joan Berlin. *Surviving the Breakup.* New York: Basic Books, Inc., 1980.

16 Weiss, Robert S. *Marital Separation.* New York: Basic Books, Inc., 1975.

17 Wheeler, Michael. *Divided Children: A Legal Guide for Divorcing Parents.* New York: W.W. Norton and Company, 1980.

## II. Journal Articles

1  Bahr, Steven J. "Mediation Is the Answer." *Family Advocate 3* (1981): pp. 32-35.

2  Carrod, David Clayton. "A Modest Proposal to End Our National Disgrace." 2 *The Family Advocate* 30 (1979): pp. 30-43.

3  Coogler, O.J. "Changing the Lawyer's Role in Matrimonial Practice." *Conciliation Courts Review* 15,1 (1977): pp. 1-8.

4  ------------; Weber, Ruth E.; and McKenry, Patrick C. "Divorce Mediation: A Means of Facilitating Divorce and Adjustment." *The Family Coordinator* (April 1979): pp. 255-259.

5  Crouch, Richard E. "The Dark Side is Still Unexplored." *Family Advocate* 4 (1982): pp. 27-35.

6  Freed, Doris Jonas, and Foster, Jr., Henry H. "Divorce in the Fifty States: An Overview." *Family Law Quarterly* XIV,4 (Winter 1981): pp. 229-283.

7  Fuller, Lon L. "Mediation—Its Forms and Functions." *Southern California Law Review* 44 (1971): pp. 305-339.

8  Gaughan, Lawrence. "Taking a Fresh Look at Divorce Mediation." *Trial* (April 1981): pp. 39-41.

9  Gold, Lois. "Mediation in the Dissolution of Marriage." *The Arbitration Journal* 36,3 (September 1981): pp. 9-13.

10  Herrman, Margaret S.; McKenry, Patrick C.; and Weber, Ruth E. "Mediation and Arbitration Applied to Family Conflict Resolution: The Divorce Settlement." *Arbitration Journal* 34,1 (1979): pp. 17-21.

11  Kelly, Joan B., and Wallerstein, Judith. "The Effects of Parental Divorce: Experiences of the Child in Early Latency." *The American Journal of Orthopsychiatry* 46,1 (January 1976a): pp. 20-32.

12  Meroney, Anne E. "Mediation and Arbitration of Separation and Divorce Agreements." *Wake Forest Law Review* 15,4 (August 1979): pp. 467-486.

13  Mnookin, Robert H., and Kornhauser, Lewis. "Bargaining in the Shadow of the Law: The Case of Divorce," *The Yale Law Journal* 88 (1979): pp. 950-997.

14  Pearson, Jessica. "How Child Custody Mediation Works in Practice." *Judges Journal* 20,1 (1981b): pp. 10-12.

15  ---------------, and Thoennes, Nancy. "Mediation and Divorce: The Benefits Outweigh the Costs." *Family Advocate* (1982): pp. 26-32.

16  Silberman, Linda J. "Professional Responsibility—Problems of Divorce Mediation." *Family Law Quarterly* XVI, 2 (Summer 1982): pp. 107-145.

17  Spencer, Janet, and Zammit, Joseph P. "Mediation-Arbitration: A Proposal for Private Resolution of Disputes Between Divorced or Separated Parents." *Duke Law Journal* 5 (1976): pp. 911-939.

18  Stulberg, Midge Cowap. "When Three is Not a Crowd." *Family Advocate* 12, 4 (1980): pp. 4-5.

19  Trombetta, Diane. "Custody Evaluation and Custody Mediation: A Comparison of Two Dispute Interventions." *Conciliation Courts Review* 19,1 (June 1981): pp. 13-20.

20  Winks, Patricia L. "Divorce Mediation: A Nonadversary Procedure for the No-Fault Divorce." *Journal of Family Law* 19 (August 1981): pp. 615-653.

## III. Magazine Articles

1 Chase, Janet. "Divorce Mediation: A Promising New Alternative to the Pain of Fighting in Court." *Glamour*, September 1983, pp. 252-256.

2 "Dealing the Lawyers Out of Divorce." *Changing Times*, June 1983, pp. 82-85.

3 Forst, Elizabeth. "Divorce Without Dueling." *McCalls*, November 1982, p. 88.

4 Gest, Ted. "Divorce—How the Game is Played Now." *U.S. News & World Report*, November 21, 1983, pp. 39-42.

5 Levine, Carol. "Divorce: Mediation or Confrontation." *Psychology Today*, November 1983, p. 20.

6 Louie, Elaine. "Upfront: The High Price of Divorce." *House & Garden*, March 1981, pp. 16 and 22.

7 Pierson, Stephanie. "The Spoils of Divorce." *Cosmopolitan*, November 1982, pp. 168, 171, and 175.

8 Porterfield, Kay Marie. "Mediated Divorce." *Single Parent*. May 1983, pp. 18-20.

9 Press, Aric; Clausen, Peggy; Burger, William; Abramson, Pamela; McCormick, John; and Cavazos, Sandra. "Divorce American Style." *Newsweek*, January 10, 1983, pp. 42-48.

10 Quaglietta, James. "Minimizing Taxes in Separation and Divorce." *The Tax Magazine*, August 1980, pp. 531-541.

11 Runde, Robert. "Cutting up the Family's Fortunes." *Money*, November 1983, pp. 147-158.

12 Vroom, Patricia; Fassett, Diane; and Wakefield, Rowan A. "Winning Through Mediation: Divorce Without Losers." *The Futurist*. February 1982, pp. 28-34.

13 Wiegner, Kathleen K. "The High Cost of Leaving." *Forbes*, Vol. 123, February 19, 1979, pp. 44-49.

14 Zakarian, Robert. "Divorce's Friendly Persuaders." *Money*, April 1980, pp. 85-87.

## IV. Newspaper Articles

1 Barbash, Fred. "Burger Urges Mediation to Ease Court Burden." *The Washington Post*, January 25, 1982.

2 Cox, Meg. "Friendlier Endings: Some Divorcing Couples Find Mediation Cheaper and More Humane than Battles in Courtroom." *The Wall Street Journal*, November 15, 1983, p. 60.

3 Mann, Judy. "Child Support." *The Washington Post*, November 23, 1983, p. C1.

# MEMORANDUM OF AGREEMENT

## Financial Disclosure

Myles agrees to a complete disclosure of the full extent of his income and property of all kinds, prior to the signing of the agreement. This will be done with the assistance of the tax consultant, _____. Myles agrees to cooperate fully with him by furnishing information and permitting examination of books and records as requested.

Myles also agrees to furnish Karen with ongoing information on the status of his estate, including his podiatry practice, author's agreements, record company and farm. He will also give her information as to the status of his will and insurance.

## Costs Of Mediation

These costs, to include the fees of the mediator, tax consultant and attorney, will be paid by Myles. He may deduct 50% of these expenses from the settlement Karen will receive under the agreement.

## Support And Maintenance

Myles will pay to Karen a monthly amount, which sum will be fixed after the tax analysis by the tax consultant. The figures set forth here are not the monthly amount, but rather the after-tax income which Karen will realize from that amount. The computations assume a unitary sum of spousal and child support under the *Lester* rule, so that the entire amount will be deductible by Myles and taxable to Karen. The tax consultant will also recommend to Myles the best way for the tax advantage to be reflected in Myles's requirements as to monthly cash flow.

For the first three years after the agreement becomes effective, the monthly sum will be _____. For the fourth year, it will be _____ and for the fifth year,_____. Thereafter it will be _____ per month until Frankie reaches age 18, then _____ per month until Sam reaches age 18, at which point it will terminate.

The sums due under this provision will terminate at Karen's death. They will, however be enforceable against Myles's estate until either Myles or Karen remarries, but not afterwards. In such event, Myles will provide a minimum of _____ insurance for each minor child, with the child as beneficiary and Karen as trustee.

If Karen remarries, the sums due under this provision will be renegotiated. The new amounts will not be less than _____ per month, nor more than _____ per month, for each minor child. The amounts will depend upon Karen's financial position as well as Myles' financial circumstances at the time.

If prior to her remarriage Karen, through no fault of her own, suffers serious financial distress, Myles agrees to assist her within the limits of his means at the time through a loan or other financial assistance.

## Real Property

Myles and Karen are owners, as tenants by the entirety, of a townhouse at _____. Karen is presently residing in this townhouse. It was purchased in 1974 and has an approximate present value of _____. The mortgage presently has an outstanding principal of _____.

Myles will transfer his one-half interest in the townhouse to Karen. _____ will advise the parties as to the means to deal with capital gains taxes on the townhouse.

In accordance with real estate custom, Myles will be responsible for the cost of the deed transferring his interest in the townhouse. Karen will be responsible for the fees of recording the deed.

After the transfer Karen will be responsible for all of the expenses of the townhouse, including principal, interest, taxes, insurance, utilities and repairs. Karen may sell the townhouse at her sole discretion.

## Personal Property

The parties will complete an agreed division of their personal effects and household items, to the extent that this has not already been done. A schedule evidencing the division will be attached to the agreement unless the exchanges have been completed when the agreement takes effect.

## Other Property Matters

Karen waives any rights she may have in any real or personal property which Myles holds in his separate name. This waiver includes any interest in his podiatry practice.

Karen agrees to execute the documents necessary to relinquish to Myles her interest in the following stocks:

_____

_____

_____

The parties agree that these stocks were the separate property of Myles and the transfer is intended to conform the title of the stocks to this fact.

Karen and Myles agree that each will have the full ownership of the automobiles in his or her possession. Each will execute any documents for the Virginia Division of Motor Vehicles which are necessary to reflect this provision. Any such document will be executed within ten days of the effective date of this agreement.

## Cash Payment To Karen

Myles will pay to Karen the sum of _____ not later than 30 days after the effective date of this agreement. Karen may use this money in any way she chooses.

## Health Insurance
Myles will maintain health insurance coverage for Karen for so long as this is possible, and for Frankie and Sam during the period they may be covered under his policy.

## College Education
Myles will be solely responsible for the financial support of Frankie and Sam after each boy reaches age 18, to continue through four years of college. This provision will apply only during the period each boy is enrolled in college. Myles agrees that he will not use the fact of this financial responsibility for the detriment of Karen's relationship with the boys.

## Custody And Visitation
Karen will have the care and custody of Frankie and Sam. Myles will have regular and frequent visitation at his residence or elsewhere.

The parties recognize that visitation should take place in a manner which will permit everybody to plan ahead. This will require reasonable prior notice if either party so requests.

In general, the boys will be with Myles every other weekend from Friday night through Sunday night, one month in the summer. Religious, national and school holidays, as well as birthdays, will be divided in an equitable manner.

The parents agree to consult each other in all important decisions affecting the upbringing and proper growth and development of the children.

# TAX CONSULTATION MEMORANDUM

This Tax Consultation Memorandum is to provide Myles and Karen Schneider with information and recommendations concerning the tax consequences and other financial aspects of their Memorandum of Agreement mediated by _____.

## Financial Disclosure—Myles Schneider
This financial disclosure is based upon review of items on Myles's and Karen's 1979 income tax return and statements from Myles. The return for 1980 has not been filed and, therefore, is unavailable. I have no reason to believe that additional assets not listed on the 1979 return or otherwise disclosed exist.

## Support and Maintenance
I am recommending the following Alimony and Child Support payments to enable Myles to maximize his cash flow while allowing Karen the full benefit of the after tax income in the first three years of the agreement during which time she does not plan to work but will be attending school. Once Karen begins employment, I have formulated a sharing of the higher tax-bracketed income by using a ratio of alimony divided by total income. My recommended provisions follow:

## Alimony
*A. Duration.* Myles (hereinafter H) will pay alimony to Karen (hereinafter W) commencing in the month this agreement is signed and ending on the earlier of (1) July 31, 1992, (2) death of H, or (3) death of W. (Actual day of payment will be determined at a later date).

*B. Amount.* Subject to all limitations in the other paragraphs under this section, "Alimony", and commencing in the month this agreement is signed, H shall pay to W _____ per month for a period of 36 months, then _____ per month during the next 12 months, then _____ per month for the next 12 months, then _____ per month through September 1990, then _____ per month through July 1992.

*C. Remarriage or cohabitation by W.* If prior to the 60th month following the month in which this agreement is signed W remarried, alimony payments immediately will reduce to _____ per month and continue in that amount through September 1990, at which time the alimony payment will reduce to _____ per month through July 1992.

*D. Death of child.* If either child, Frankie or Sam, dies prior to attaining 18 years of age, the monthly alimony payment due under paragraph B or C of this section, "Alimony", shall be reduced in the amount of _____ with respect to the death of each child.

*E. Additional alimony.* Commencing in 1982, in addition to the alimony payments due under the other paragraphs of this section, "Alimony", on April 1st, June 1st, September 1st, and December 31st of each calendar year H shall pay alimony to W in the amount necessary to enable W to pay estimated tax payments to the Federal and State government. Such estimated tax payments will be calculated as if the alimony payments due under this agreement are the sole source of income of W. In addition, commencing in 1983, on or before April 7th of each calendar year H will pay alimony to W in the amount determined by the following formula:

[Alimony paid under this agreement for the previous calendar year divided by the total income received by W during such year and required to be included as taxable income for such calendar year (in 1980, this amount would appear on line 22 of Form 1040)] times [Tax liability for such calendar year after taking into account any tax credits but not including any tax liability resulting from "other taxes" (in 1980, other taxes are listed on lines 48-53 of Form 1040)] less [The amount paid under this paragraph listed as being due April 1st, September 1st, and December 31st of such calendar year]

[Note: A projected tax return for Karen in 1982 is attached]

## Child Support
*A. Duration.* H will pay child support to W for the support and maintenance of each child, Frankie and Sam, commencing in the month the agreement is signed and ending on the earlier of (1) the month the child attains 18 years of age, (2) the death of the child, (3) the death of H, or (4) the death of W. [Actual day of payment will be determined at later date]

*B. Amount.* The amount of child support shall be _____ per month for each child.

*C. Dependency exemption.* H and W agree that H shall claim the dependency exemption for each child for every tax year following the year in which this agreement is signed, however, if in any tax year the Internal Revenue Service determines that H is not entitled to claim the exemption for either child, then W may claim the exemption for such tax year if W is so entitled.

## Life Insurance *(p. 1 of Memorandum of Agreement)*
I recommend that Myles maintain policies in the amounts of _____ for each child as primary beneficiary and _____ for Karen as primary beneficiary for the duration of the life of the beneficiary of the term of payments under this agreement, whichever is the lesser period of time. Term insurance on the life of Myles would satisfy this provision and be relatively inexpensive to maintain. That portion of the agreement that permits Karen a claim against the estate of Myles for alimony under the settlement agreement should be deleted. Basis: money received as proceeds under a life insurance policy is tax free to the recipient, whereas, a claim against the estate for alimony may be considered taxable income when paid.

## Remarriage Clause *(p. 2 of Memorandum of Agreement)*
I recommend deletion of the clause concerning renegotiation of the agreement upon remarriage in favor of the alimony and child support provisions set forth above.

Neither party currently contemplates remarriage in the foreseeable future. The differentiation in the amounts involved is not significant (_____ per month in after tax dollars). Given Myles's potential earning capacity, I believe continued payment in the higher amount is justified in light of the agreement setting forth only minimal child support provisions.

## Other Property Matters *(p. 2&3 of Memorandum of Agreement)*

A conveyance of Karen's interest in the stocks, bonds, etc. listed is a taxable disposition. The existence of any gain or loss should be ascertained before the settlement agreement is signed. I do not believe that Karen has any interest in Myles's podiatry practice and the relinquishment of any interest, if any exists, therein should be sufficiently covered by the usual release of dower claims and release of interest in "all property held solely by the other" clause. Again this may result in a taxable disposition, but this type of general clause has not been determined to have any actual ascertainable value to my belief.

## Health Insurance *(p. 3 of Memorandum of Agreement)*

Coverage for Frankie and Sam may be maintained by Myles under a family policy. This will only be true of Karen until a divorce decree is granted. Although the parties do not contemplate a divorce decree at this time, tax consequences dictate this be obtained before December 31, 1982 to allow the parties to file as being single. Only as "a mensa" decree is necessary to allow this. If Myles is unable to maintain a family policy that includes Karen upon the granting of a final divorce decree, then the burden will shift to Karen to obtain health insurance. This may determine whether an "a mensa" decree or a final divorce decree is obtained in 1982. Rules of Myles's health insurance carrier should be examined as well as the cost of an individual policy for Karen.

## Children's College Education *(p. 3 of Memorandum of Agreement)*

Whether this is intended to give a contractual right to the children as third party beneficiaries should be addressed in the final agreement. Pro: security for the child for education and incentive to obtain that education. Con: right to payment for education regardless of cost and performance of child.

## Custody *(p. 4 of Memorandum of Agreement)*

I recently have been involved with a problem concerning a client (non-custodial father) whose daughter has come to live with him in Virginia. Although he has been taxpaying resident of Virginia for more than five years, the state supported university she plans to attend maintains that she is an out of state student because he is not the custodial parent. The increase in tuition costs will be well over $1000 per year. To relieve this potential problem, perhaps the agreement should state joint custody for Myles and Karen coupled with a clause that the children will reside with Karen until attaining 18 years of age. The negative aspect of joint custody may be a potential for tort liability of the "non-residential" parent for the tort of the minor child. I do not know of any case law on this point, I only conjecture. Perhaps _____ will have some insight into the pros and cons of joint custody.

## Tax Returns

Myles and Karen will file joint Federal and State income tax returns for 1981. Beginning with calendar year 1982, an "a mensa" decree or final divorce decree should be obtained and Myles will file as Single and Karen will file as Head of Household. If a Gift Tax return is necessary as concerns the townhouse, Myles will be required to file this as well. The recent tax law changes may be determinative of this.


Respectfully submitted,

# CUSTODY, PROPERTY AND SEPARATION AGREEMENT

This agreement is made and entered into and is to take effect this _____ day of _____, 1982, by and between MYLES SCHNEIDER (hereinafter referred to as "Myles") and KAREN SCHNEIDER (hereinafter referred to as "Karen"), together sometimes referred to as "the parties".

## Preamble

Myles and Karen are presently husband and wife. They were lawfully married in Hempstead, New York, on July 9, 1967. Two children were born of this marriage, to-wit, Franklin E. Schneider, born September 15, 1972 and Samuel M. Schneider, born July 5, 1974.

Myles and Karen have decided to live apart. Each of them shares with the other the responsibility for this decision and neither holds the other to be at fault.

Myles and Karen have entered into this agreement through mediated negotiation. Each has disclosed to the other the full extent of his or her income, expenditures, real and personal property, other assets and liabilities. They intend that this agreement set forth a comprehensive and final settlement of the matters between them existing by reason of their marriage.

Now, therefore, in consideration of the exchanges and mutual promises set forth in this agreement, Myles and Karen hereby covenant and agree as follows:

## Nature And Scope Of Agreement

The parties intend that this agreement set forth their present understanding in its entirety. There are no written or oral promises between them which they presently wish to exchange but have been excluded from this Agreement.

The parties have arrived at this agreement through their mutual efforts and with the assistance of a trained and impartial mediator. Neither of them has received separate legal advice in the negotiation or drafting of this agreement. Each party is aware of the right to consult his or her individual legal counsel, and each of them chooses to waive that right.

This agreement has been carefully reviewed by each of the parties before signing. Each party represents that it does convey the joint agreement reached through mediation.

Each party acknowledges that this agreement is his or her free and voluntary act, arrived at without pressure and on full mutual disclosure of the facts. Each is satisfied that it is a fair and reasonable settlement.

## Law Governing

The parties intend that this agreement be interpreted and enforced under the laws of the Commonwealth of Virginia. They understand that if the agreement is incorporated in a divorce decree, its provisions may be enforced as a court order.

## Separate Lives

Myles and Karen shall lead their separate lives and continue to live separate and apart from each other. Each shall be free from the interference and control of the other in his or her personal life. Neither shall subject the other to restraint, censure or harassment. They shall each enjoy independence from the other in professional and social relationships.

The parties agree to treat each other with the respect and consideration appropriate to two persons who, although now living apart, have shared an important part of their lives. Nothing in this agreement shall prevent a reconciliation between them should the parties jointly desire to resume their marital relationship.

## Waiver Of Estate

Each party hereby waives and relinquishes any and all rights he or she may have to share as spouse in the other party's estate or to act as the legal representative thereof. It is the intention of the parties that this provision shall serve as a mutual waiver of the right of election to take against each other's Last Will and Testament under the present or future laws of the State of Virginia, or any other jurisdiction.

## Custody And Visitation

The parties have carefully weighed the question of custody of their children. In doing so, they have been guided solely by considerations of the childrens' welfare. They are convinced that the childrens' best interests require that Karen be their sole custodian with the most liberal rights of visitation for Myles. The parties feel that child rearing is a joint venture that requires the active participation of both parents. Therefore, even though Karen shall be solely responsible for financing the childrens' activities, the parties shall consult with each other concerning all matters of policy involving the children, such as their health, education, choice of trips, summer camps, etc., with a view to adopting a harmonious policy best calculated to promote the interests of the children. The parties shall exert every reasonable effort to maintain free access and unhampered contact between each of them and the children. Neither of them shall do anything to hamper the natural development of the children's love and respect for the other party.

In general, the children shall visit with Myles every other weekend from Friday night through Sunday night, and one month during the summer. Religious, national and school holidays shall be divided in an equitable manner. However, it is also understood and agreed that this arrangement may be subject to many exceptions and alterations. Thus, the parties may make different arrangements at any times which are mutually satisfactory to them and which are in the interests of the children. The parties shall deal amicably in good faith with each other in making the arrangements contemplated by this paragraph.

It is acknowledged by the parties that the foregoing arrangements are facilitated by the fact that the parties now live near to each other in the Northern Virginia area. The parties agree that they consider it important to continue this arrangement and they will endeavor to do so. In the event, however, that it should become necessary for either party to move to a greater distance or out of the Northern Virginia area altogether, the parties will make living arrangements for the children which will result in their spending reasonable amounts of living time with each party.

## Support

Myles agrees to pay to Karen for her support and maintenance and the support of the parties' minor children the sum of _____ per month, due and payable on the first day of each and every month, beginning February 1, 1982. The _____ payment shall be reduced to _____ per month on February 1, 1985, then on February 1, 1986 to _____ per month then on February 1, 1987 through January 31, 1992, the support payments shall be _____ per month. The payments shall terminate on Karen's death or 10 years and one day from the date of this agreement, whichever occurs first. In addition, Myles shall pay all of the state and federal income taxes that Karen may owe as a result of her receiving the support and maintenance from Myles to but not in excess of the sum of _____ per year. Myles shall make a quarterly payment to Karen of these tax monies, and said quarterly payment shall cease on the earlier of Karen's death or 10 years and one day from the date of this agreement, whichever occurs first.

Karen acknowledges that the monies paid by Myles to her for her support and maintenance and the support of the parties' minor children are taxable as income to her and are a tax deduction to Myles.

Myles shall be solely responsible for the financial support of Frankie and Sam after each boy reaches age 18, including the cost of college through an undergraduate and graduate degree.

Myles shall also pay to Karen the sum of _____ per month per child or _____ as child support for Franklin and Samuel.

Myles shall claim Franklin and Samuel as dependents on his federal and state tax returns and Karen agrees not to file a tax return in which she claims the children as dependents.

Myles may claim Franklin and Samuel as dependents even though he does not contribute over one-half of the actual expenses of the children in any taxable year.

## Insurance

Myles shall maintain a major medical insurance policy for the children until they reach the age of majority, complete their higher education, or are married or otherwise become emancipated, whichever comes first. Myles shall also maintain two life insurance policies of _____ each on his life. Franklin E. Schneider shall be the beneficiary of one of the policies and Samuel M. Schneider shall be the beneficiary of the other policy.

Myles shall also maintain a major medical insurance policy for Karen until the parties are divorced, if possible.

## Divorce
Nothing herein contained shall be construed to bar or prevent either party from suing for absolute divorce in any competent jurisdiction. This agreement, if acceptable to the court, shall be incorporated by reference in the divorce decree that may be granted in any such divorce action. Notwithstanding such incorporation, this agreement shall not be merged in that decree, but shall survive the same and shall be binding and conclusive on the parties for all time.

## Real Property
The parties presently own as tenants by the entirety the following real property: a house located at _____, present value _____. The parties agree as follows with respect to the disposition of that property. Myles and Karen recognize that the law of the Commonwealth of Virginia gives Karen certain rights of dower or other similar rights, and that these rights give Karen a vested interest in the realty jointly acquired during her marriage to Myles. Therefore, in view of Karen's willingness to release these rights in the _____ property, Myles hereby transfers to Karen all of his right, title and interest in the aforesaid _____ property. The payment will be made in the form of a deed executed by Myles to Karen at the time that the parties execute this Agreement.

The periodic payments of real estate taxes, mortgage payment, property insurance and other expenses of maintenance on the _____ property shall be paid solely by Karen so long as she retains the property.

## Personal Property Of The Parties
The parties agree to a separate, equitable and equal division of the personalty which they own as tenants by the entirety with the full common law right of survivorship. The parties have arrived at this Agreement as they both understand that under a number of principals, including Virginia case law, the equal division of jointly held property has been held to be a non-taxable event. The parties acknowledge that they have heretofore divided up between them all their personal property to their mutual satisfaction, including but not limited to the property described below. Henceforth, each of them shall own, have and enjoy, independently of claim or right of the other, all items of personal property of every kind, now or hereafter owned or held by him or her, with full power to dispose of the same as fully and effectually, in all respects and for all purposes, as if he or she were unmarrried.

(a) **Specifically, the bank account** at _____, current balance _____ shall be the exclusive property of Karen. The savings account at the _____, current balance _____ shall be the sole and exclusive property of Myles. Myles shall also pay to Karen the sum of _____ minus one-half the cost of the legal services that were provided by the mediator and counsel who prepared this Agreement.

(b) **Stocks and Bonds**—The parties currently own securities. These securities shall be the sole and exclusive property of Myles, and pursuant to the equal division of jointly-held property, Karen transfers all of her right, title and interest in the securities to Myles. The securities include the following: _____

_____

_____

_____

(c) **Automobiles**—The 1981 Ford Mustang automobile, shall be the sole and exclusive property of Myles and Karen relinquishes all of the right, title and interest that she may have in that automobile pursuant to the equal division of jointly-held property.

The 1974 Ford Pinto and the 1981 Pontiac automobiles shall be the sole and exclusive property of Karen and Myles relinquishes all his right, title and interest in those automobiles.

The parties have reviewed the division of property as set forth above, and are in complete agreement that it is fair and just.

## Modification

No waiver or modification of any of the terms of this Agreement shall be valid unless in writing and executed and done with the same formality of this Agreement. No waiver of any breach of fault hereunder shall be deemed a waiver of any subsequent breach or fault under this Agreement of the same of similar nature.

## Debts

Each party shall be responsible for their own debts and each shall not incur any debts that are or may become the responsibility of the other party.

## Arbitration

Any dispute arising out of this Agreement shall be referred to the mediation team of _____ and _____ for resolution. The parties shall abide by the mediator's decision.

**In Witness Whereof,** the parties hereunto have affixed their signatures.

_____

_____

# FINAL DECREE OF DIVORCE

Virginia:

IN THE CIRCUIT COURT OF FAIRFAX COUNTY

MYLES SCHNEIDER
Complainant.

v.                                        IN CHANCERY NO. 78964

KAREN SCHNEIDER
Defendant.

## Final Decree of Divorce

This cause came on to be heard upon the Amended Bill of Complaint; upon defendant's Answer to said Amended Bill of Complaint; upon the testimony of complainant and his witness duly taken in support of his Amended Bill of Complain before the Honorable _____, Esquire, Commissioner in Chancery; and upon the Report of said Commissioner; and

UPON CONSIDERATION WHEREOF, and it appearing to the Court, independent of the admissions of either party in the pleadings or otherwise, that said parties were lawfully married in Hempstead, New York, on July 9, 1967; that two children were born of the aforesaid marriage, namely, Franklin E. Schneider, born September 15, 1972, and Samuel M. Schneider, born July 5, 1974, which children are in the care and custody of defendant; that both parties hereto are over the age of eighteen years, and that neither party is a member of the Armed Forces of the United States; that complainant was, at the time of the institution of this suit, and for more than six months immediately prior thereto, an actual *bona fide* resident and domiciliary of Fairfax County, Virginia; that the parties hereto last cohabitated as husband and wife in Fairfax County, Virginia; that on or about January 15, 1981, the parties began to live separate and apart, and that said separation has continued without any cohabitation and without interruption from that time to the present; that there is no possibility of a reconciliation between the parties; that this Court has jurisdiction to hear and determine the case; that the parties hereto have entered into a Separation and Property Settlement Agreement dated June 3, 1982, settling their personal property rights, as well as providing for the maintenance and support of the parties and custody and support of said minor children of the parties hereto, which Agreement and Amendment are filed herein, it is therefore

**ADJUDGED, ORDERED and DECREED** that the complainant, MYLES SCHNEIDER, be and he hereby is, awarded a Final Decree of Divorce *a vinculo matrimonii* from the defendant, KAREN SCHNEIDER, on the ground that the parties hereto have lived separate and apart, without any cohabitation and without interruption, for a period of more than one year next preceding the institution of this action, and the bonds of matrimony heretofore existing between the parties are forever dissolved; and it is further,

**ADJUDGED, ORDERED and DECREED** that the terms of the parties' Separation and Property Settlement Agreement dated April 20, 1982 and Amendment to said Agreement dated June 3, 1982, be and the same hereby are, affirmed, ratified and incorporated into this Decree, to the extent permitted pursuant to Section 20-109.1 of the Code of Virginia (1950 ed., as amended), and the parties are hereby ordered and directed to comply therewith, and it is further

**ORDERED,** that the Clerk of this Court furnish forthwith certified copies of this Decree to counsel for complainant and defendant.

AND THIS DECREE IS FINAL

ENTERED this _____ day of _____, 1982


_____
JUDGE

BY:

_____
Counsel for Myles Schneider

SEEN:

_____
Karen Schneider

# MARITAL MEDIATION RULES

**Section 1 Agreement of Parties to Mediate.** The parties shall be deemed to have made these rules a part of their mediation agreement whenever their agreement so provides or whenever they have agreed in writing that mediation shall be conducted by a facility certified by the Family Mediation Association. These rules and any amendment thereof shall apply in the form obtaining at the time the mediation is initiated. Certified fcilities are hereinafter referred to as "Center," and Family Mediation Association as "FMA."

**Section 2 Mediation of Future Dispute Under Contract Provision.** A provision for mediation under these rules in either an antenuptial contract or a settlement agreement may be initiated in the following manner:

    a. The initiating party may give notice to the opposite party of his intention to mediate, which notice shall contain a statement setting forth the nature of the dispute including the amount involved, if any, and the remedy sought, and

    b. By filing with a center two copies of said notice together with two copies of the mediation provisions of the contract.

    c. The center serving as administrator shall give further notice of such filing to the opposite party. If the opposite party so desires, an answering statement in duplicate may be filed with the center, in which event a copy of the answering statement shall be sent to the initiating party by the center. If the opposite party fails to file an answer, mediation shall proceed at a time and place fixed by the center not earlier than ten days after mailing a notice to both parties.

**Section 3 Scope of Mediation.** Any mediation process constituted by the parties under these rules, unless otherwise stipulated, shall be related to fostering settlement and resolving controversies between them concerning one or more of the following matters, to wit: division of property; custody of minor children including visitation, child support, spousal maintenance; cost of mediation and arbitration; and attorney's fees.

**Section 4 Mediation Situations.** Mediation under these rules shall be applicable in the following situations.

    a. When the parties are husband and wife and have reached a decision to live separately.

b. When the parties are husband and wife, have reached a decision to live separately, and either one or both parties have decided on, or are considering the dissolution of their marriage. The decision to dissolve or not dissolve the marriage shall not be an issue for mediation.

c. When the parties are divorced and a controversy exists between them regarding modification of a previous decree of the court and it is contended that there has been a change of circumstances justifying such modification.

**Section 5 Administration.** When parties agree to mediation under these rules, and designate a certified center, they thereby constitute the center as the administrator of the mediation. The authority and obligations of the administrator are prescribed in these rules. In the event the parties shall fail to agree upon or designate a particular center, FMA shall designate a center as administrator, and its decision shall be final and binding.

**Section 6 Panel of Marital Mediators.** The FMA shall establish and maintain certified panels of marital mediators from which mediators shall be appointed.

**Section 7 Appointment of Mediator.** Upon receipt of notice of intention to mediate under Section 2 of under an agreement under Section 1, the center shall appoint a mediator or mediators for the parties.

**Section 8 Number of Mediators.** Mediation shall be conducted by a single mediator, unless either party shall request that there be two mediators before the first mediation session. In the event two mediators are requested, one shall be male and the other shall be female.

**Section 9 Qualifications of Mediators.** Mediators shall be neutral in their relationship to the parties and shall disclose to the center any circumstances likely to create a presumption of bias, or any financial or personal interest in the result of the mediation or any past or present relationships with either of the parties or persons closely related to them. Upon receipt of such information from the mediator or other source, the center shall communicate such information to the parties and, if it deems appropriate to do so, to the mediator. Either party or the mediator may request that he be replaced at any time, giving the center reasons therefore. The center shall determine whether a mediator should be disqualified or replaced and shall inform the parties of its decision which shall be conclusive.

**Section 10 Vacancies.** If any mediator should resign, die, withdraw, refuse appointment, be disqualified, or for any other reason shall fail to consistently perform the duties of his office, the center may declare the office vacant. Vacancies shall be filled in accordance with the rules regarding appointment of mediators.

**Section 11 Appointment of Advisory Attorney.** The parties may select from FMA's panel of approved attorneys an advisory attorney at law with whom arrangements can be made to provide impartial legal advice needed for reaching settlement. The parties may also select any other attorney mutually acceptable to them, provided he acknowledges in writing appointment as an impartial advisory attorney under these rules and agrees to abide by them in serving the parties. The center shall appoint an advisory attorney from the panel upon the failure of the parties to make a selection or at their request. The advisory attorney shall be compensated at an hourly rate acceptable to the parties in advance of appointment.

**Section 12 Obligations of Advisory Attorney.** The advisory attorney, by accepting appointment, undertakes the following obligations:

a. He will advise the center and the parties of any circumstance which might create a presumption of bias on his part in favor of or against either party.

b. He will under no circumstances accept professional or other employment, or the promise thereof, from either party so long as their marital dispute is unresolved and during a period of one year thereafter. By mutual agreement of the parties, he may represent one of them for the sole purpose of obtaining a decree of separation or divorce which incorporates the settlement agreement reached by the parties under these rules.

c. He will, as fully as possible within the time available, explain to each party in the presence of the other party and the mediators his and her rights and obligations under the law.

d. He will give particular attention to the tax consequences resulting from the various options available to the parties in reaching settlement.

e. He will maintain strict impartiality in his advice to the parties and will refrain from attempting to influence either party toward making a particular decision or settlement.

f. After preparation of a settlement agreement, he will fully and impartially explain its terms to each party in the presence of the other and the mediators, and will answer questions to the best of his professional abilities.

g. He will communicate with the parties only in mediation sessions or through the center of the mediators and in no other manner directly or indirectly. Further, he will immediately report to the mediators any attempt on the part of a party to communicate with him and advise the party of his obligation.

h. He shall make known to the parties and mediators in advance the maximum number of hours of professional time he expects to render outside of mediation sessions for preparation of the settlement contract of legal research.

i. An advisory attorney may spend only the number of professional hours authorized by the parties.

j. He shall have an attorney-client relationship with the parties and will regard all communications and information obtained during mediation as privileged.

k. The motivations of the parties in reaching a decision to separate or to dissolve their marriage are matters to be dealt with by marriage counselors or other properly qualified therapists and do not come within the purview of the mediation and arbitration processes.

**Section 13 Compensation of Mediators.** Each mediator shall be compensated at an hourly rate not exceeding that approved by the center under FMA policies and which is acceptable to the parties.

**Section 14 Certification and Supervision of Centers.** Centers offering mediation under these rules may arrange with FMA for certification and supervision during certification.

**Section 15 Mediation Fee Deposit.** Upon filing of the agreement for mediation under these rules (Section 1 or 2), the center may require that the parties deposit an amount of money sufficient to cover the following items:

a. Ten hours for mediator's fees
b. An additional estimated amount from which the advisory attorney's fees and/or paraprofessional legal services may be paid

During the mediation process, as the deposit becomes depleted, the center may require that the parties make additional deposits so as to maintain adequate funds needed to continue the mediation process without interruption.

**Section 16 Refund of Deposit.** The unused portion of deposits provided for in the preceding section shall be refundable to the parties as follows:

a. When settlement has been reached and executed in writing by the parties.
b. If, during mediation, a party becomes permanently disabled or deceased or the parties become reconciled and resume their marital relationship.
c. When impasse has been reached, as provided in Section 20, and the parties are proceeding with arbitration.
d. In the event the parties shall fail or refuse to proceed with mediation and/or arbitration after ten (10) days' written notice has been mailed to them, all deposits remaining become the property of the center and FMA in equal shares.

**Section 17 Communications with Mediators and Advisory Attorney.** The parties shall not communicate with the mediators or advisory attorney concerning matters in mediation except in the presence of each other during a mediation session. In the event either party shall violate or attempt to violate this rule, the mediator or attorney shall have the duty to ask such party to refrain from such communication and to thereafter promptly report such communication to the center. Communications regarding the scheduling of appointments are permitted under this section.

**Section 18 Cancellation of Appointments.** Notice of cancellation of mediation appointments must be given by the parties to the center not less than 24 hours in advance of the appointment. Otherwise full charge may be made for the appointment not kept.

**Section 19 Attendance at Mediation Sessions.** The parties shall arrange their business and personal affairs so as to provide for attending mediation sessions once each week.

**Section 20 Determination of Impasse.** *Impasse* is defined as a situation resulting when the parties and the mediators have examined as fully as appears useful all information and options reasonably available for reaching settlement of an issue and the parties fail to reach an agreement. The failure or refusal of one or both parties to abide by these rules shall also constitute an impasse when so determined by the mediator. The mediators or a party may declare that an impasse has been reached as follows:

a. By the mediator at any time.

b. By a party with the concurrence of the mediator in advance of completion of ten hours of mediation time.

c. By a party with or without the concurrence of the mediator after completion of ten hours of mediation time.

**Section 21 Confidentiality of Mediation.** By undertaking mediation under these rules, the center and the parties mutually agree with one another as follows:

a. Mediation is a procedure for reaching settlement of a dispute either in litigation or likely to be in litigation between the parties.

b. All communication between the parties and with the mediators and the center related to the dispute shall come within the purview of the rules of evidence which exclude from introduction in evidence by either party against the other disclosure made with a view to settlement.

c. The parties shall be estopped through their adoption of these rules from calling either the mediator or any officer or agent of the center as a witness in litigation of any description in which they are called upon to testify as to any matter regarding the mediation proceeding; and the parties shall be estopped from requiring the producing in court of any records or documents or tape recordings made by the mediators or the center.

d. The foregoing exclusions from evidence and exemptions of the mediators and parties from giving testimony or being called upon to produce documents shall apply in the same manner to arbitration of an impasse.

e. Mediations conducted by a licensed professional shall come within the purview of his professional privilege.

**Section 22 Tape Recording of Mediation Sessions.** The center may require that mediation sessions be recorded subject to the following conditions:

a. In the absence of written consent of the parties, audiotape recordings will be heard only by the parties, the mediator, and the mediator's supervisor if he is subject to supervision.

b. Mediators shall disclose to the parties at the beginning of mediation whether or not the mediation sessions will be subject to audiotape supervision.

c. Except as above stated, audiotape recordings are strictly confidential and shall not be used for research, training, or any other purpose without prior written consent of the parties, and then in such manner as does not disclose the identities of the parties.

d. Videotape recordings shall be made only with the prior written consent of the parties.

**Section 23 Full Disclosure.** Each party shall fully disclose, in the presence of the other party, all information and writings, such as financial statement, income tax returns, etc., requested by the mediator and all information requested by the opposite party if the mediator finds that the disclosure is appropriate to the mediation process and may aid the parties in reaching settlement.

**Section 24 Preparation of Budgets.** The preparation of budgets by each party, when either spousal maintenance or child support or both are claimed, is an essential part of the mediation process. If either party shall fail or refuse to prepare a budget adequately reflecting his needs, the mediator shall have the duty to suspend mediation of these issues or, at his discretion, declare an impasse.

**Section 25 Participation of Children and Others.** Children for whom custodial arrangements are being made and other persons having a direct interest in the mediation may participate in mediation sessions related to their interests, if the mediator finds that their participation may facilitate settlement.

**Section 26 Third-Party Involvement.** During the mediation process, the parties shall refrain from discussing the matters in mediation with all third parties including friends, relatives, and attorneys, and with each other except as directed by the mediators.

**Section 27 Temporary Custody and Support-Arbitration.** At the first mediation session the parties will reach agreement, if possible, with regard to temporary custody and temporary support for the minor children, temporary support for the spouse seeking maintenance, attorney's fees, and the cost of mediation and arbitration. In the event the parties shall not reach agreement in whole or in part, the mediators shall declare that the parties are in impasse. Upon notification by the mediators that the parties are in impasse, the center shall appoint a single arbitrator who will fix a time and place for hearing not later than seven days after impasse is declared and, after hearing from each party who appears, shall render an award fixing temporary spousal maintenance, temporary custody and support of minor children, the cost of mediation, arbitration, and attorney's fees. The agreement reached between the parties, or the award of the arbitrator, and the provisions of Section 28 of these rules may be made an order of the court having jurisdiction upon the petition of either party without further advance notice or service upon the opposite party.

**Section 28 Transfers of Property.** During the mediation and arbitration process under these rules, neither party shall transfer, encumber, conceal, or in any other way dispose of any tangible or intangible property except in the usual course of business or for the necessities of life. Proposed transactions by either party in the regular course of business or for any other purpose affecting 10 percent or more of the total assets of a party shall be reported to the other party not less than ten days in advance of the transaction contemplated. Transactions made in violation of this rule shall be subject to being declared void and set aside upon the application of the injured party, either in arbitration under these rules or in a court of competent jurisdiction.

**Section 29 Temporary Court Order.** During mediation or arbitration, either party may request a court of competent jurisdiction to issue a temporary injunction without requiring advance notice to the opposite party:

  a. Restraining any party from transferring, encumbering, concealing, or
     in any way disposing of any property except in the usual course of
     business or for the necessities of life and, if so restrained, requiring him
     to notify the moving party of any proposed extraordinary expenditures
     and to account to the court for all extraordinary expenditures made
     after the order is issued.

b. Enjoining a party from molesting or disturbing the peace of the other party or of any child.

c. Excluding a party from the family home or from the home of the other party when there is evidence that physical or emotional harm would otherwise result.

**Section 30 Guidelines for Division of Property.** The parties shall reach agreement providing for the division of marital property with the assistance of the mediators, without regard to marital misconduct, in such proportions as is just, after considering all relevant factors, including:

a. The contribution of each spouse to the acquisition of the marital property, including the contribution of a spouse as homemaker.

b. The value of the property to be received or retained by each spouse.

c. The economic circumstances of each spouse at the time the division of property is to become effective, including the desirability of awarding the family home or the right to live therein for reasonable periods to the spouse having custody of any children.

d. Any increases or decreases in the value of the separate property of each spouse during the marriage or the depletion of the separate property for marital purposes.

e. For purposes of this section:
*Active ownership* of property is inferred from the owner's making capital improvements, usage, management, and other efforts intended to enhance the value of the property.
*Passive ownership* is inferred from the absence of facts of which would result in an inference of active ownership.
*Marital property* means all property acquired by either spouse subsequent to the marriage except:

(1) Property acquired by gift, bequest, devise, or descent.

(2) Property acquired in exchange for property acquired by gift, bequest, devise, or descent.

(3) Property acquired by a spouse after a decree of legal separation.

(4) Property excluded by valid agreement of the parties.

(5) The increase in value resulting from passive ownership of property acquired prior to the marriage, or after the marriage by gift, bequest, devise, or descent.

(6) When increases in value of property acquired prior to the marriage, after the marriage or by gift, bequest, devise, or descent have resulted from both active and passive ownership, a reasonable allocation shall be made so as to exclude increases attributable to passive ownership.

f. All property acquired by either spouse after the marriage prior to a decree of legal separation or divorce and all increases in value attributable to active ownership of property whenever or however acquired,

f.  All property acquired by either spouse after the marriage prior to a decree of legal separtion or divorce and all increases in value attributable to active ownership of property whenever or however acquired, are presumed to be marital property regardless of whether title is held individually or by the spouses in some form of co-ownership, such as joint tenancy, tenancy in common, tenancy by the entirety, and community property. The presumption of marital property shall be overcome by a showing that the property or increase in value of property is excluded under the provisions of the preceding subsection.

g.  Property shall be valued for purposes of this section as of the date of the first mediation session.

**Section 31 Spousal Maintenance Guidelines.**  Payment of maintenance by one spouse to the other shall be predicated upon the following considerations as they apply to the spouse seeking maintenance:

a.  The spouse lacks sufficient property, including marital property apportioned to him, to provide for his reasonable needs.

b.  The spouse is fully or partially unable to support himself through appropriate employment or is the custodian of a child whose condition or circumstances make it appropriate that the custodian not be required to seek employment outside the home.

c.  Maintenance shall be in such amounts and for such periods of time as is just, without regard to marital misconduct and after considering all relevant factors, including the following:

(1)  The financial resources of the party seeking maintenance, including marital property apportioned to him, and his ability to meet his needs independently, including the extent to which a provision for support of a child living with the party includes a sum for that party as custodian.

(2)  The time necessary to acquire sufficient education or training to enable the party seeking maintenance to find appropriate employment

(3)  The standard of living established during the marriage, reduced by the impact that maintaining two households rather than one may have upon the standard of living of the parties

(4)  The duration of the marriage

(5)  The age and physical and emotional condition of each spouse

(6)  The ability of the spouse from whom maintenance is sought to meet his needs while meeting those of the spouse seeking maintenance

**Section 32 Child Support Guidelines.**  Either parent or both parents, according to their ability to do so, shall accept the duty of support for a child of the marriage and contribute an amount reasonably necessary after considering all relevant factors, including:

a. The financial resources of the child

b. The earning ability and financial resources of each parent

c. The standard of living the child would have enjoyed had the marriage not been dissolved, reduced by the impact that maintaining two households rather than one may have upon the standard of living of the parties

d. The physical and emotional condition of the child and his educational needs

**Section 33 Child Custody Guidelines.** In reaching agreement regarding custodial arrangements reflecting the best interests of the child, the parties shall consider all relevant factors, including:

a. The wishes of each parent as to the custody of the child

b. The wishes of the child as to custodial arrangements

c. The interaction and interrelationship with his parent or parents, his siblings, and any other person who may significantly affect the child's best interests

d. The child's adjustment to his home, school, and community

e. The mental and physical health of all individuals involved

The conduct of a parent that does not demonstrably affect his relationship with the child, or in some other way can be shown to be contrary to the best interests of the child, shall not be considered.

**Section 34 Rights of the Custodial Parent.** The custodial parent may determine the child's upbringing, including his education, health care, and religious training, except as otherwise agreed by the parties. The custodial parent shall have the right to require that the noncustodial parent follow agreed visitation with the children on a consistent and dependable basis.

**Section 35 Rights of the Noncustodial Parent.** The noncustodial parent of the child shall be entitled to reasonable visitation rights such as do not adversely affect the child's education or physical health or significantly impair his emotional development. The noncustodial parent shall carry out visitation arrangements as a privilege and obligation of parenthood and to share parenting responsibility with the custodial parent.

**Section 36 Rights of Joint Custodial Parents.** Joint custodial parents agree to establish a cooperative relationship with each other regarding the exercise of their continuing responsibilities as parents of their children. They accept that each has an equal right to determine the child's upbringing, including his education, health care, and religious training. The child's living arrangements between the two parents shall be such as are in the best interests of the child, using as guidelines the provisions of Section 33 of these rules. Even though joint custody reflects a cooperative attitude on the part of both parents, specific living arrangements shall be included in the settlement agreement. Such arrangements shall be followed except as are otherwise agreed upon by the parents from time to time. The living arrangements contained in the settlement agreement shall not be changed by such subsequent agreements. Either parent on notice to the other may reestablish the arrangements contained in the settlement agreement.

**Section 37 Controversy Over Custody.**  At the first mediation session, the mediators shall determine whether the parties are in agreement regarding custody of the minor child or children. In the event custody of the children is in controversy, the mediator shall advise the parties that mediation of the custody issue shall be the last item on the agenda after agreement has been reached upon all the following:

a. Division of marital property
b. Spousal maintenance
c. Child support
d. Attorney's fees for the petitioning spouse when the parties contemplate dissolution of their marriage.

The mediator shall further instruct each party to prepare two budgets—one based upon the assumption that he is the custodial parent and a second based upon the assumption that he is the noncustodial parent.

**Section 38 Agreement upon Issues during Mediation.**  As agreement is reached upon each issue during mediation, the mediator shall determine that the parties understand the agreement reached. Thereafter, the same issue shall not be reopened for mediation, after a new issue is taken up, without authorization by the mediator. The mediator shall grant authorization to reopen mediation of an issue to the extent needed to correct mistakes or to consider new information which was not reasonably available to one or both parties previously.

**Section 39 Execution of Settlement Agreement.**  The advisory attorney shall personally supervise the execution of the settlement agreement reached by the parties during mediation. Such agreement shall be prepared and submitted to the parties when one of the following situations arises:

a. The parties have reached settlement of all issues.
b. The parties have reached settlement of all issues except custody (including visitation) which will require further mediation.
c. The parties have reached settlement of some issues and are in impasse over others, in which case the agreement shall reflect the issues agreed upon and shall clearly specify the position of each party regarding issues in impasse.
d. The parties are in impasse over all issues, in which case the agreement shall clearly specify the position of each party in each issue.
e. The failure or refusal of either party to enter into the agreement provided for in Subsections c and d shall not limit the other's right to proceed with arbitration.
f. A supplemental or revised agreement shall be executed reflecting custodial arrangements agreed upon after further mediation, as provided for in Subsection b above.

**Section 40 Evaluation of Settlement Agreement.**  In advance of their execution of the settlement agreement, either party may request that a special evaluation session be scheduled. At such evaluation session, the mediator and the advisory attorney shall offer the parties their opinions as to the overall workability of the proposed agreement, pointing out the advantages and disadvantages to each party. To the best of their ability and on the basis of their previous experience, the mediator and attorney shall indicate whether the agreement is substantially consistent with agreements reached by couples similarly situated.

**Section 41 Concurrence of Mediators.** The mediators may indicate to the parties their concurrence or nonconcurrence with the settlement agreement reached. A written notation of the mediators' concurrence or nonconcurrence shall be made below the signatures of the parties on the settlement agreement and shall be signed by the mediators. Concurrence indicates the mediator's judgement that the settlement appears to be substantially equitable and fair to each party. Nonconcurrence shall in no way detract from the legal effectiveness of the settlement contract reached between the parties.

**Section 42 Arbitration.** The parties shall submit to arbitration all controversies which are the subject of mediation under these rules when impasse is reached under Section 20 of these rules. Arbitration shall be conducted under the Marital Arbitration Rules of the FMA and in accordance with applicable statutory arbitration laws of the state in which the arbitration is conducted. The parties accept the jurisdiction of the court competent to handle divorce cases, in the place where the arbitration is conducted for all purposes related to the conduct of the arbitration, such as compelling the attendance of witnesses and the production of documents. The parties shall faithfully observe this provision for arbitration and the arbitration rules, so that the award rendered by the arbitrators shall become a part of the settlement agreement reached between the parties, and/or that such award may be entered in and made the judgement of any court having jurisdiction thereof.

**Section 43 Masculine and Feminine Gender.** Whenever in these rules the masculine gender is used, it shall be understood to include the feminine unless the context clearly indicates otherwise.

**Section 44 Interpretation and Application of Rules.** The mediator shall interpret and apply these rules. In the event of a controversy between the mediator and the parties regarding interpretation or application of these rules, such questions shall be referred to the center for a decision which, however, shall be subject to review by FMA.

**Section 45 Amendment of Rules.** FMA reserves the right to amend these rules at any time, provided, however, such amendment shall not apply to the rules included in mediation agreements relating to existing controversies. The rules as amended and in force at the time notice of intention to mediate is given under Section 2 shall apply in mediations under agreements to mediate future disputes.

# INDEX

## A

Accountant, independent, 50, 55, 58
See also Tax consultants
Adversarial system, 23-7
Children and money as weapons,
24;
Exacerbation of conflicts, 24-25;
Lawyers and negotiation, 23-24;
Versus mediation, 29-30;
Why people turn to, 26-27
Agreements, 49;
Divorce decree, 50-51;
Mediator concurrence, 70;
Memorandum of non-concurrence,
70-71;
Separation, 50, 51, 57, 77,
136-140, 143, 156, 166
Tax consultation memorandum,
136, 146;
Temporary support and custody,
49
Alimony. See Spousal support
American Arbitration Association, 48;
For help finding mediator, 64, 66
American Bar Association, 64;
For help in finding a mediator, 64,
65
Arbitration, 198-199, 205;
Definition of, 72;
For impasse resolution, 48, 55,
59-60, 73, 76, 77
Attorneys, advisory, 196-197;
Choice of, 137;
Fees, 48, 57, 67;
Independent, 50, 55, 58, 77;
Role of, 43, 49-50, 57, 68, 69, 72
79, 138-141, 165

## B

Bank accounts, 107-108

## C

Child custody and visitation, 150-154;
Area of contention, 43;
As part of mediation agenda, 49,
55-56;
Children's participation, 73;
Definition of, 46-47;
In California courts, 63;
In other courts, 64;
Mediator's experience with, 66;
Modification of, 78;
Our sessions pertaining to, 81-86;
Spousal manipulation of, 24
Child support, 154-158;
Area of contention, 43;
As part of mediation agenda, 49,
55-56;
Changes in payments, 156-157;
Compliance/non-compliance, 155-
156;
Definition of, 45-46;
How determined, 154, 155;
Modifications, 78;
Our sessions, 129-136;
Tax implications of, 157
Communication skills, 90-92, 94
Conciliation, 71-72;
As part of negotiation, 93
Conflict, 87-89;
Definition, 87
Conflict resolution, 66;
As part of mediator's training, 69;
As part of negotiating, 88-89;
Strategies of, 88-89

Coogler, O.J., 27
Courts, 64;
    Conciliation, 64, 65, 176;
    Domestic Relations, 64;
    Family, 64–65;
    Juvenile, 64'
    Of competent jurisdiction, 77, 78;
    Probate, 64
Credit cards, 108
Custody, 150–154;
    Children's role, 152–153;
    Definition of, 150–151;
    Finality of arrangements, 153–154;
    Joint, 151;
    Split, 151;
    Vacation arrangements, 153;
    Who gets, 151–152

**D**

Divorce decree, 50, 137;
    Mediator's non-concurrence with,
        71, 137, 141;
    Our own, 193–195
Divorce, definition of, 87
Divorce mediation. See Mediation
Divorce Mediation Research Project,
    65;
    National directory for mediation
        training, 66;
    National listing for divorce
        mediators, 65

**F**

Family Mediation Association, 42;
    Confidentiality of mediator and
        mediation, 71;
    For certification of mediators, 66;
    For finding mediator, 64;
    Purpose of, 42;
    Specialized mediation association,
        65;
    Training by, 43
Financial disclosure, 76, 199–201;
    Legal recourse to force, 162;
    Our sessions pertaining to, 97–104,
        132–136;
    See also, Taxes, Child support,
        Spousal support

Financial information, 105–128;
    Budgets, 44;
    Data, 44, 47, 48–49, 106;
    Forms, 47, 57, 100, 101;
    Statements, 44, 57, 76;
    See also, Taxes, Child support,
        Spousal support

**I**

Insurance policies, 108

**L**

Lawyers, see Attorneys
Lester Rule, 139;
    Lesterizing, 157

**M**

Marital mediation rules, 195–205;
    As guide when impasse occurs, 48;
    Marital mediation based on, 42;
    Our sessions, 129–132;
    Part of orientation, 47, 54–55;
    Regarding children, 73;
    Role of mediator, 69–70; 71, 73–74
Marital property, 160–163;
    Area of contention, 43;
    As part of mediation agenda, 49,
        55–56
    Debts, 163;
    Definition of, 44–45, 76;
    Distribution of, 161;
    Laws pertaining to division of, 78;
    Long term debts, 163;
    Pension funds as part of, 107;
    Retirement funds as part of, 107;
    Tax implications, 160–162;
    Value of, 161–162
Mediation, marital, 41–50;
    Agenda, 49, 73;
    An alternative approach, 12–13;
    Areas of contention, 43;
    Cost of, 16, 48, 57, 59, 67, 68;
    Definition of, 27–28;
    Family oriented, 29;
    Impasses, 48, 55, 60, 73, 76,
        198–199;
    Is it for you?, 14–16, 74–76;
    Orientation session, 47;

Purpose of, 41–42, 50;
Results of, 28–29, 42, 77;
Versus adversarial system, 29–30;
Who assists couple, 43
Mediators, 196–198;
Background of, 52, 53, 66;
Concurrence with agreement, 70, 137;
Non-concurrence with agreement, 70–71, 137;
Role of, 43, 44, 52–55, 68–71, 73–74, 77–78, 89, 137–142, 146–148;
Training, 66
Memorandum of agreement, 136;
Concerning child support, 156;
Mediators role with, 137–140;
Review our own, 143, 146, 165, 181–183

## N

Negotiation, 87–96;
Communication skills of, 90–92;
Definition of, 87–89;
Pitfalls of, 92–93;
Techniques of, 89–90, 93–94

## O

Orientation, 47;
Packet of materials, 47, 51

## P

Pension and retirement funds, 107;
Part of marital property, 107
Personal information sheet, 48–49

## S

Separation agreement, 140–141;
Our own, 148, 188–192
Sessions, 47, 49, 52–58;
Costs of, 67;
First, 49, 52;
Orientation, 47–49;
Later ones, 49;
Length of, 72;
Location of, 72;
Special evaluation, 138;
Tape recordings of, 71

Spousal support, 158–160;
Area of contention, 43;
As part of mediation agenda, 49, 55–56;
Changing amount of, 159;
Definition of, 45;
How enforced, 158;
Modification of, 78;
Our sessions regarding, 129–136;
Tax implications, 159–160;
Who gets, 158–159
Stocks and securities, 108;
Tax exempt bonds, 108
Support, rehabilitative, 45;
Spousal, see Spousal support

## T

Tape recording, of mediation process, 71;
Confidentiality of, 78
Tax consultants, 43;
Fees of, 48, 57, 67;
In our sessions, 136, 143–146;
Role of, 49, 138–140
Tax consultation memorandum, 136;
Our own, 146, 184–187
Taxes, 107;
Advantages of mediation, 131–138, 139–140, 143–146;
Implications of child support upon, 157; of marital property upon, 160–162; of spousal support upon, 159–160;
Requesting copies of returns, 107;
State returns, 108